P9-DUF-433

Get Great Marks For Your Essays

Get Great Marks
For Your Essays

John Germov

ALLEN & UNWIN

Copyright © John Germov 1996

All rights reserved. No part of this book may be reproduced
or transmitted in any form or by any means, electronic or
mechanical, including photocopying, recording or by any
information storage and retrieval system, without prior
permission in writing from the publisher.

First published in 1996 by
Allen & Unwin Pty Ltd
9 Atchison Street, St Leonards, NSW 2065 Australia
Phone: (61 2) 9901 4088
Fax: (61 2) 9906 2218
E-mail: 100252.103@compuserve.com

National Library of Australia
Cataloguing-in-Publication entry:

Germov, John.
    Get great marks for your essays.

    Includes index.
    ISBN 1 86448 158 7.

    1. English language–Rhetoric. 2. Report writing.
    I. Title.

808.042

Set in 10.5/12pt Garamond and Optima by DOCUPRO, Sydney

Printed by Australian Print Group, Maryborough, Vic 3465

Contents

Acknowledgments

I thank my friend and colleague, Lauren Williams, for contributing the mindmapping sections and providing invaluable input in reviewing the manuscript throughout its development. Steve Campitelli's cartoons add the necessary good humour which I hope academics and students always keep in mind. Thanks also for the support I have received from my colleagues in the Department of Sociology and Anthropology at the University of Newcastle. I especially want to thank my partner, Sue Jelovcan, without whose help, encouragement and enthusiasm this book would never have been written. Final thanks go to my publisher, Elizabeth Weiss, for her professionalism, encouragement and support.

Introduction: what this book can do for you

Have you ever wondered why students are made to write essays? What are essays and why are academics so fussy about how they are done? Does it all seem unnecessarily highbrow and complex? If you have ever asked yourself such questions, then this book is for you! This book provides a 'user friendly' guide to researching, writing and referencing tertiary essays. No matter which discipline or subject you study, or whether you are a University or TAFE student, this book will reveal the secrets of getting good marks.

The content of this book is based on the points I have found useful in teaching students over the years. It is designed to answer the most common questions and problems students encounter when writing essays by giving practical examples and handy hints. Writing essays can be a frustrating and confusing task. However, the whole process can be made easier once you understand the rules, expectations and standards required.

This book has been designed with four broad categories of students in mind:

- the student who needs to know what is expected of a tertiary essay
- the mature age student who may not have written an essay for a long time
- the student who is not good at writing essays, but would like to improve his or her skills
- experienced students wanting to jog their memory or improve their essay technique.

There are many individual styles in researching and writing essays, and different departments and disciplines also have specific requirements. However, the essentials of essays stay the same no matter what subject you do. Whilst this book will show you handy hints to save time, there is no easy way to 'beat the system'. What this book offers is a number of insights and skills which you can use to make the task of writing essays easier.

THE STYLE OF THIS BOOK

This book is written in an informal way to make it easy to understand. Therefore, it uses contractions (can't, we've) and a chatty, conversational style of writing. In contrast, tertiary essays require a *formal* style of writing, which this book will explain and show you how to achieve.

HOW TO USE THIS BOOK

This book can be read from cover to cover or, for the more experienced, you can dip into various parts which may interest you by scanning the contents and index pages.

Whichever way you use this book, it is structured so that you do not have to read lengthy slabs of writing, with plenty of practical examples to put the words of advice into action.

ESSAY FLOWCHART

The flowchart below depicts the various stages of the essay writing process. The rest of the book explains how best to go about each stage of the writing process.

Chapters 1 and 2

↓

- The standards expected of a tertiary essay
- Understanding and choosing an essay topic

Chapters 3 and 4

↓

- Planning an essay
- Brainstorming
- Doing analysis

Chapters 5 and 6

↓

- Researching information and taking organised notes

Chapters 7, 8 and 9

↓

- Drafts 1, 2, 3 . . .
- The art of writing and handling the nitty-gritty

Chapter 10

↓

- Referencing checklist

Chapters 11, 12 and 13

↓

- Writing reports, exam essays, abstracts and summaries
- Editing and proofreading
- Essay submission checklist

1

First things first: introducing the academic detective

This chapter describes what is expected of you in a tertiary essay. It explains why you are made to write essays and offers some handy hints about organising your essay writing time.

Your essay is almost due and all you have is an essay topic with a few brief instructions. If you're lucky, you may have had a tutorial on some basic essay techniques but that's it! No-one has really told you what is expected, what you lose and gain marks on, and how much effort or time you are expected to put in. This chapter will help to clarify all of these matters.

THE ACADEMIC DETECTIVE: WHAT IS AN ESSAY ANYWAY?

Why are you made to go through the torture of writing essays? What is an essay meant to achieve as an assessment task? Let me answer these questions with an example. Essays involve a lot of detective work. Think of yourself

The academic detective.

as an academic detective who is on the lookout for facts, motives and logical explanations. This means putting aside any personal views you may have about a topic and searching for the evidence and evaluating the differing explanations or theories. In your quest for understanding and explanation you are to leave no stones unturned. This involves adopting a 'critical eye'. The academic detective accepts nothing on blind faith. An essay is the product of your research. It is not just a log of your efforts, but shows your understanding of the topic and your evaluation of theories which attempt to explain the issue or problem you have investigated. Detective work can be lonely and frustrating, but there are methods you can use to help your investigation along. The first thing you need to come to grips with is the level or depth at which to pitch your detective efforts.

INTO THE GREAT UNKNOWN: WHAT'S EXPECTED OF A TERTIARY ESSAY?

Many students are often ill-prepared for writing tertiary essays and experience a great shock when their first essay is returned with a lower than expected mark. There is a jump in the standard of work required when you move from a secondary school to a tertiary institution. Often, this great leap forward is into the unknown because few teachers actually spend much time telling students what's expected of them and how to go about meeting those expectations. Academics expect students either to have essay skills or to be able to acquire them miraculously in a very short time.

The tertiary essay differs from what you may have written in secondary school in a number of ways:

- you are expected to read widely in order to review critically the field of literature on a topic. Copying information from a single book is not acceptable
- you are expected to write analytical essays which are not just descriptive, but attempt to explain issues often via the use of theories
- you are expected to support what you say by supplying evidence
- you are expected to source the content of your essay by some form of referencing system which shows where you got the information from.

Essays are not an easy assessment task, but they can be a task over which you have the most control. At the undergraduate level, an essay usually does not need to be based on original research or even original thought. You are not expected to come up with the answers to the world's problems in 2000 words, especially when people have often written books on the topic! Essays are about learning; showing proof of your research effort, your knowledge and your understanding of the topic. The tertiary essay is based on the following skills:

- independent thinking (this means no-one will tell you exactly what to do)
- finding, selecting, organising and referencing information
- analysing information from competing explanations and sources
- answering a question in a given time frame and word limit.

Essay writing skills extend beyond the walls of the education system into later life. Contrary to popular belief, essays are not some form of perverse initiation ritual designed to make life hard for students. Many jobs require you to write letters, memos, reports and information sheets for clients, all of which to greater and lesser degrees require research, referencing and organisational writing skills. The tertiary essay is therefore the training ground for future life and employment skills. It is a tool for communicating your knowledge and your understanding. Most importantly, essay writing teaches you to think by giving you the skills to analyse a topic systematically and communicate your 'thinking' about the topic in a logical way.

ORGANISE YOUR TIME

The early bird

The first mistake you can make is to dive headlong into the essay, before you have a clear idea of what's involved. An essay is not something you can just start and make up as you go along. Planning and research are everything: if you don't get this part right, the rest of the essay will not fall into place and you'll be left panicked and confused as the due date approaches. There are ways to avoid such pitfalls. First some handy hints to organise your mind. At the start of the semester make a list for all of your subjects of what work is due and when, and keep it handy (see example opposite). Just putting the due date in your diary may not give you enough warning unless you constantly flip through your diary ahead of time. As often happens, you may forget and flip over the page only to see something is due tomorrow! The example below shows a fictional list of work due.

Example:	Plan for your assignment due dates
March	12: SOC120 Tutorial presentation 28: PSY101 In-class essay exam
April	15: POL102 Book review—800 words 15: HIS112 Essay—2000 words
May	10: POL102 Essay—1200 words 20: SOC120 Essay—2000 words
June	12: PSY101 Exam 15: SOC120 Exam

Once you have compiled your list of work due, make sure you allow yourself plenty of time to do your essay. As the example above shows, it is not uncommon to have two items of work due in the same week, even on the same day. Making a list of your assignment due dates allows you to plan ahead in such situations. You are expected to be able to handle a number of assignment tasks at the one time, so an early start is essential. You should allow a few weeks to work on each essay, on and off. By giving yourself plenty of time, you avoid the mad rush for library books in the two weeks prior to the due date and are therefore more likely to get the sources of information you want. It will also give you time to consult your tutor.

There are a number of other reasons why it is best to start early on your essay. It is important that you put a lot of thought into the essay before you start to write it. Your essay is *your* answer to a specific question or issue. Therefore, you need to consult a variety of written sources to become acquainted with information, research, theories and criticisms; and appraise the collected material: what is relevant or irrelevant, supported or unsupported, tentative or conclusive? All of this takes time.

Writing is a skill that improves with practice. By writing a few drafts you will find that your expression and essay structure become clearer and more concise each time. You should allow enough time to produce at least three drafts of your essay. Be patient. It is important that you take the time to:

- plan your essay
- find information
- understand your reading
- put information in your own words and link it logically.

How much effort, how much time?

Students are often unclear about how much effort and time they should put into an essay. The figure will vary according to the discipline and the nature of the task, but for the standard tertiary essay of 2000 words, students at first year level are expected to do a minimum of 20 hours of work to complete the essay. Don't panic! This time includes doing research, reading and note taking, producing essay drafts and the final version for submission.

Only use this figure as a guide; *it is a minimum.* Your lecturers and tutors may expect you to do much more—even double the hours!—So ask them what they expect.

BE PROACTIVE: ASK QUESTIONS

If in doubt, ask your tutor or lecturer for clarification of the essay topic. It is quite acceptable for you to ask questions about your assessment tasks to ensure you have a clear idea of what is expected of you. Often essay topics can be broad, with many books written on a subject, so it's easy to go off on a tangent. Tutors are there to help you, so ask questions for clarification, either in class or after class. If you have specific questions relating to your essay and your reading, then either 'phone your tutor in her office or make an appointment to see her.

When meeting with your lecturer or tutor do some thinking and preliminary reading before you arrive. There is nothing academics dislike more than a student who makes an appointment to see them about an essay, but has done no work and has nothing to say. Lecturers and tutors are not there to do your essay for you and spell out every issue to be covered in a 'join the dots' approach to writing essays. By all means be proactive and ask questions, or show a plan or draft of your essay to your tutor. However, do not arrive with an empty slate expecting her or him to fill in the blanks. Keep the following two steps in mind to ensure you keep on track.

1. Always write for your intended audience. Be sure to write essays containing the information, theories and debates relevant to the subject and discipline. For example, if you are doing sociology and psychology subjects, do not try to rehash your psychological material for your sociological essay unless it is particularly relevant. Whilst many topics cross over discipline boundaries, it is much simpler to stick to identified books and journal articles within the one discipline. It is a simple rule to follow: if it is a politics subject, use politics texts; if it is an economics subject, use economic texts. In other words, always write for your intended audience. It is the only way to ensure you have covered the material relevant to the topic. The example below compares how the same essay topic should be written for different disciplines.

2. Sample essays. If you are unsure about how to write an essay in a particular discipline, ask to see some sample essays. This is not an unreasonable request. Lecturers and tutors will often have samples of good essays from previous students and they will be happy to let you have a look at them in order to gain an understanding of what is expected of you in the subject.

Essay topic: How does social class affect the lives of Australians?

History essay. How have the perceptions and evidence of class changed over time? What influence has class had on Australians over time, such as during the depression in the 1930s or during and after the world wars?

Politics essay. What class differences exist between the political parties in terms of who votes for them, their policies, and their philosophies? Do various classes exercise power over government and individuals in Australia?

Sociology essay. What evidence of class exists? Is there a ruling class and an underclass? What theories explain class? Can there be a classless society? How important is class compared to other forms of inequality such as gender or racial inequality? How does a person's initial class position affect his or her chances of social mobility, health, education, wealth?

Psychology essay. Do Australians perceive class as important in their lives? What behavioural differences exist between classes? Does class influence individual values which in turn affect the motivations of people from different classes to stay healthy, do well at school and at work? How do various psychological theories attempt to explain class differences in values and behaviour?

Handy hint: use a subject folder

It is useful to keep a subject folder. Use one folder for each subject, in which you should keep all of your lecture, reading and tutorial notes. Your subject folder will help with studying, especially for exams. Bring it to lectures and tutorials so that all of your notes are kept in one place. An alphabetically indexed section at the back of your folder is also useful for keeping the definitions of terms you come across in lectures, tutorials and reading all in one place. It will save you time having all definitions in one place instead of having to search through a semester's lecture and tutorial notes.

2

The rules of the essay writing game

This chapter maps out the structure of an essay. It introduces you to the various rules of the game of essay writing which will help you to create logical and well reasoned essays.

Each academic detective has his or her own style in going about the search for clues in order to answer an essay question. However, there are some rules which all good academic detectives follow. An essay is like a game. A game has certain rules which you have to follow if you want to play and have a chance of winning. Once you have learnt the rules, you have a good chance of success.

STICK TO THE RULES

When marking your essay your tutor will expect it to keep to the rules of the game—that is, to follow a conventional or accepted format. The tertiary essay is expected to have the following (all of which are covered in the various chapters of this book):

- an introduction, body of evidence and conclusion (have you answered the question?)
- logical flow
- clear argument
- appropriate length
- referencing and bibliography
- correct grammar and spelling.

STRUCTURING AN ESSAY IN THREE PARTS

An essay is made up of three parts: a beginning, a middle and an end. In its simplest form, an essay is meant to:
- tell your audience what you *intend* to tell them (the introduction)
- *tell them* (the body of the essay)
- tell them what you *have* told them (the conclusion)

Most people know this, but the skill is in writing these sections well and linking them together.

An essay in three parts.

Tell them what you intend to tell them: introducing the topic

Some people write introductions last, others can't start an essay until the introduction is written. Either method is fine, but because your essay will change from one draft to the next your introduction will need to reflect this, so leave the final version of your introduction until last. Avoid simply restating the essay question in your introduction and instead interpret the topic and outline the major issues and explanations or theories to be discussed. Introductions are usually between half a page and one page long, depending on the essay length and the complexity of the topic. Introductions are meant to clarify the topic so that the reader can anticipate and understand what lies ahead in the rest of the essay. Introductions should do four things:

1. Tell the reader what your essay is about by interpreting the question or topic.
2. State what the essay will cover.
3. Outline what the essay will argue (how to develop an argument is explained in Chapter 4).
4. Provide definitions of key words or concepts contained in the essay question.

In the example below, note how the introduction clearly defines what the essay is about and outlines what will follow in the body of the essay.

Example: An essay introduction

Essay topic: Examine the links between social class and health status.

This essay will focus on health inequalities and examine the relationship between social class and health status. Despite the existence of welfare programmes and equal opportunity legislation, there is clear evidence that the working class has considerably poorer health. Evidence of the links between class and health will be given and then conservative theories of inequality will be contrasted with a Marxist class analysis in an attempt to explain why health inequalities persist.

In the above introductory paragraph, note how the student has introduced the topic and stated what the essay will cover. Since there is some debate over what class is and how many classes there are, the next paragraphs will need to define class, especially what is meant by working class, before presenting the evidence and various theoretical explanations. **Note that this is not the only way of writing the introduction in this case, but the example does cover the basics of what introductions should do.**

Tell them: the body of your essay

The body of an essay has two features: description and analysis (sometimes called explanation). This is where you present your case; the evidence you have amassed from your detective work based on your reading as well as the explanations of the issues you are dealing with. It is important to show how your information is relevant to the essay topic. To continue the example of the essay topic on class and health, the body of the essay could cover the following:

Example: the body of the essay

- A summary of the evidence of class and its effects on health status (the working class tend to have a lower life expectancy due to the nature of manual work). This summary represents the descriptive part of the body of the essay.
- The next part of the body of the essay needs to analyse the descriptive evidence through a review of the major theories which attempt to explain *why* there are links between class and health.

Tell them what you've told them: the conclusion

The conclusion summarises what you have told your reader, emphasising the key points of your argument in order to answer the question. For example, in concluding the essay on class and health, you could write the following:

Example: the conclusion

As discussed in this essay, conservative theories rely on ideology rather than evidence to support their case. Recognising the clear links between class and health shows how social, economic and political factors influence health status, where some individuals are less sick than others. Solutions to address inequalities in health status need to focus on the way work is organised, regulated and monitored.

Resist the temptation to introduce new information in the conclusion which looks like an afterthought and will cause the marker to wonder why you did not mention it in the body of the essay.

ESSAY STRUCTURE

Markers often complain that student essays lack a clear essay structure. What they mean is that the material presented is not connected in a logical way. Often essays are full of disconnected sentences and paragraphs because the student has not had a clear idea of what the essay is about. Whilst the content is there, it is presented in a haphazard, almost scattergun way, jumping all over the place from one point to another with little linkage between sentences and paragraphs.

The way to create a clear structure is through the correct use of paragraphs, especially the correct use of topic and linking sentences. To ensure that your essays are logically put together, you need to know what essay structure is all about. The essay skeleton on the next page depicts the structure all essays should follow.

Making the logic flow: micro-essay paragraph structure

Developing essay structure is really quite easy, but it takes practice. The trick is to treat each paragraph in your essay as a micro-essay. Just like your essay, each paragraph should have an introduction, body and conclusion.

The *introduction* to your paragraph is known as the topic sentence (see the essay skeleton). Topic sentences simply summarise or introduce what you are going to say in your paragraph.

The *body* of the paragraph then expands on this sentence by providing definitions, evidence and further explanation. Often the body of the paragraph contains an example to emphasise the main point introduced in the topic sentence.

The *conclusion* of the paragraph is known as the linking sentence, which simply links the paragraph to the next paragraph. You normally do this automatically, but when dealing with complex information and issues, and especially when cutting and pasting sentences and paragraphs from one part of your essay to another, it is easy for the logical structure of your micro-essays (the paragraphs) to disappear.

The essay skeleton

Introduction

State what your essay is about, what it will cover and what you will argue. Define all key words and limit essay scope if necessary. Usually one paragraph, but can be longer depending on essay length.

Topic sentence

The topic sentence introduces the issue to be dealt with in the paragraph, followed by supporting evidence, explanation, and a linking sentence to the next paragraph.

Linking sentence

Topic sentence

Linking sentence

Topic sentence

The body of your essay is where you introduce your evidence, and compare and evaluate concepts and theories.

Linking sentence

Conclusion

Sum up your essay content and argument. Ensure that you answer the question. Mention possible solutions or future implications if appropriate.

It follows from the above that paragraphs cannot be one or two sentences long. The use of many one or two sentence paragraphs is a tell-tale sign that the micro-essay structure is missing. Conversely, paragraphs should not be a page or more in length. Remember, paragraphs generally contain one major point which is defined, clarified and supported with evidence.

Read the example below and look for the micro-essay structure of the paragraph—that is, the introduction (topic sentence), body (supporting evidence) and conclusion (linking sentence).

Example: the micro-essay

Essay topic: Examine the links between social class and health status.

This essay will focus on health inequalities and examine the relationship between social class and health status. Despite the existence of welfare programmes and equal opportunity legislation, there is clear evidence that the working class has considerably poorer health. Evidence of the links between class and health will be given and then conservative theories of inequality will be contrasted with a Marxist class analysis in an attempt to explain why health inequalities persist.

In the above example, the student introduces what the paragraph is about in the first line (the topic sentence).

The next sentences expand on the first, by providing greater detail and explanation (the body).

The final sentence concludes the paragraph by indicating the next major point to be discussed, providing the link to the next paragraph. See the 'Handy hint' box for some examples to help with writing linking sentences and paragraphs.

The micro-essay.

Subheading caution

The use of subheadings in an essay is a matter of individual preference. In general, avoid the use of subheadings for relatively short essays (below 3000 words). Subheadings are best used to break up lengthy text, especially when it may not all be read in one sitting. The danger in using subheadings in your essay is that you might fail to provide proper topic and linking sentences. Even when you use subheadings, your micro-essay structure should stay intact—that is, your paragraphs should still be linked together in a logical flow. Abuse of subheadings results in a disjointed essay and loss of marks. The rule of thumb when using subheadings is that you must not use them as an excuse for not linking what comes before and after the heading. The essay must still maintain a clear structure.

Handy hint: linking sentences and paragraphs

Intensify as a matter of fact, in fact, in any case, in any event, it can be seen that

Give examples for example, for instance, an illustration, in particular, to demonstrate

Compare similarly, equally important, likewise

Show addition again, finally, another reason, furthermore, moreover, consequently

Contrast although, yet, in contrast, on the contrary, however, in spite of, despite

Summarise in brief, in summary, in other words, finally, accordingly, as a result

3

We need a plan

This chapter shows you how to figure out what an essay topic is about and how to plan what to write. It shows you some good techniques to get started, particularly if you are a little confused or unsure about what the essay topic is about.

Too many students jump head first into an essay without really having an idea of where they're going. For a tertiary level essay, you cannot rely on writing off the top of your head nor can you rely on one text or just your lecture notes. There are no short cuts, so don't place yourself in a situation in which you are desperate enough to try to find them. The key to all essays is a good plan. Your plan may change over time as you do more research or begin to write up your notes, but all good essays start with a clear plan. Spending time on this stage of the writing process will actually save you time later because you will have clarified what your essay is about, what information you need to find and what the basic structure of your essay should be.

Writing off the top of your head.

CHOOSING AN ESSAY TOPIC

Many subjects offer you a range of essay topics to choose from. If this is the case, try to choose a topic that will keep your interest throughout the writing of the essay. At the start of semester, it is difficult to select a topic when you know very little about the subject. To see whether you are interested in a topic you can either wait for the related lecture, or do the preliminary reading on it either from your textbook or a list of references if provided. If this does not help, go to the library and look up some information on the topic. The key thing to keep in mind is the importance of knowing what the essay topic is about before you choose it. Do not choose a topic simply because it looks easy. Some essay topics will be more applied whilst others will be more theoretical, but all this is taken into account when the essay is marked. Go through the preparatory stage of finding out about a topic first so that you don't start working on an essay topic only to find you hate it and need to change topics mid-stream.

Once you have chosen a topic, it is time to plan your course of action. There are three stages to planning an essay:
1. the thinkplan: defining and limiting the scope of a topic
2. brainstorming ideas
3. developing your argument.

STAGE 1: THE THINKPLAN

The thinkplan is the first stage of your essay plan. It basically involves doing some initial reading on the essay topic and thinking about what your essay should cover, before you make a detailed essay plan. So before you start researching your essay you need to thinkplan—that is, understand what your essay topic or question is asking you to do. Your lecture notes, textbook or prescribed reading list are the best places to start. At this stage do not do extensive reading; leave this until after you have an essay plan. The thinkplan involves three inter-related parts: *command words, key words* and *essay scope.*

Command words

Questions will often have 'command words', such as *discuss, compare, analyse*, which direct the approach you should take to the topic. Two examples are provided below:

Discuss the implications for employees of the new industrial relations reforms.

Compare the various theories which attempt to explain social inequality.

Also, be aware of any directions which limit the topic to specific areas, such as:

Compare *two* theories which attempt to explain social inequality.

Discuss how the new industrial relations reforms affect *manual* workers in *Australia*.

A word of caution. Whilst most *command words* are quite straightforward, it is my experience that lecturers often have different things in mind when they use such words as *compare or analyse*. Ask your lecturer or tutor what the essay is expected to cover. The 'Handy hint' box below should help you understand the most commonly-used command words.

Handy hint: command words defined

Analyse. Do not describe/summarise events. Your main focus should be on the 'why' or 'how' of a particular issue, aiming to clarify reasons, causes and effects.

Compare. Find similarities and differences between two or more ideas, events or theories. Ensure you understand exactly what you are being asked to compare.

Contrast. Same as above, but you should concentrate on *dissimilarities*.

Criticise. Assess the merit of the factors being considered. Discuss both strong and weak points and give the results of your analysis.

Define. Provide concise and clear meanings. Briefly cite the boundaries or limitations of the definition.

Describe. Present facts, processes or events. You are not asked to explain or interpret. Try to provide a thorough description, emphasising the most important points.

Discuss. Present a point of view. This will need both description and analysis. Your opinion must be supported by evidence.

Evaluate. Present a judgment of an issue by stressing both strengths/weaknesses and advantages/disadvantages.

Explain. See analyse above.

Key words

Each discipline has its own jargon that you will be expected to learn. Highlight, circle or underline the key words in the essay topic which need to be defined and explained.

For example, the following terms may appear in humanities and social science essays:

conflict theory	best practice
gender	psychoanalysis
class	historical revisionists
division of labour	discourse
post-modernism	infrastructure
cultural relativism	ethnocentrism

To find out what these key words mean, start with discipline dictionaries. However, your understanding should not be based on these alone, as the meanings of specific terms are often subject to debate and are more complex than a few lines in a dictionary can allow. Introductory texts are also a good place to start to give you a basic understanding of the key words. *Do not* use literal definitions of words from dictionaries such as the Oxford or Macquarie dictionaries. You need to understand how the particular discipline—be it education, sociology, economics, literature, psychology or politics—defines the key words, because often they have more complex and specific meanings than standard dictionaries allow. For example, if you used the Macquarie dictionary to define the phrase 'division of labour', you could define 'division' (split into parts) and 'labour' (the act of working). However, such a definition adds nothing to your essay and ignores the meaning of the phrase within the disciplines of sociology, politics or economics. Within these disciplines, 'division of labour' can mean the division of productive tasks as in a system of mass production, which some theorists believe unnecessarily leads to boring and dull work.

Essay scope: sticking to the 'define and narrow'

Once you have defined and understood your command and key words, it is important that you use these words as a guide to your research and reading. You may find that there is so much information or so many issues involved in the essay topic that it is impossible for you to cover them all adequately within the word limit you are given. In such cases, without changing the meaning of the essay topic, it may be acceptable for you to narrow the scope of what you will cover in the essay. For example, this may mean concentrating on Australian issues only, or comparing two opposing theories. However, check with your lecturer or tutor that this is an acceptable practice.

STAGE 2:
BRAINSTORMING—MAPPING OUT YOUR PLAN

Once you have a general understanding of the topic and your definitions of key words, and have done some initial reading, the next stage is to plan what you need to say in the essay. Start with a blank sheet of paper and write down anything that comes to mind regarding the topic—all the ideas, issues, theories, arguments and evidence you are aware of. This is called visualisation: by actively writing what you know on paper, you clarify and organise the information in your head and what you will do with it. You may alter, modify, add to, or reject various aspects after further reading, but brainstorming allows you to go over the basic ideas your essay will cover. If you find you have little to go on, do some further reading and then come back to brainstorm. There are two ways of doing this, one of which should suit you:

1. the linear plan
2. mindmapping.

The linear plan

The linear plan involves writing your essay plan in the order it will appear in your essay. See the example below.

Essay topic: Discuss the socioeconomic status of indigenous people in two countries.

Command words. 'Discuss' means 'describe and analyse'.

Limit scope. Australia and New Zealand (Aboriginal and Maori indigenous peoples).

Key words. Define 'socioeconomic status' and the two 'indigenous peoples'.

Brainstormed ideas. Evidence of social inequality: wealth, poverty, health, education, social mobility, discrimination.

- Explanations and comparison: why there are similarities and differences.
- Evaluate the strengths/weaknesses of the various explanations/theories.
- What are the current policies/possible solutions to address the socioeconomic inequalities?

The limitation of the linear method is that you might get stuck on which order the various sections should go in. The alternative technique overcomes this limitation.

Mindmapping

Mindmapping is a diagrammatic representation of your thinking or brainstorming on paper. Mindmapping is a purely creative process allowing an uncensored flow of ideas from your mind to paper. To do it you start with your essay topic in a 'bubble' in the centre of a blank page.

Compare the socioeconomic
status of indigenous people
in two countries

Then think about what you need to include in the
essay, not in any order, just as it occurs to you and write
it in a bubble radiating from the central idea.

Compare the socioeconomic
status of indigenous people
in two countries —————— Australian and
New Zealand
evidence

Keep adding these 'bubbles' until you have everything
that needs to be covered in the essay somewhere on the
page (see page 28).

Now you can study your mindmap and think about
the best logical sequence for your essay. Number the
bubbles to put the sections in sequence (see page 29).

As mentioned earlier, this technique will appeal to
some people, whilst others will prefer a linear plan. The
advantage of mindmapping is that you separate the creative
activity from the editing activity and this saves you time
by allowing the creative juices to flow uninterrupted. More
on mindmapping can be found in Chapter 7.

Once you have formed an outline of what you want
to say, it is time to consider your argument and begin to
research the various sections.

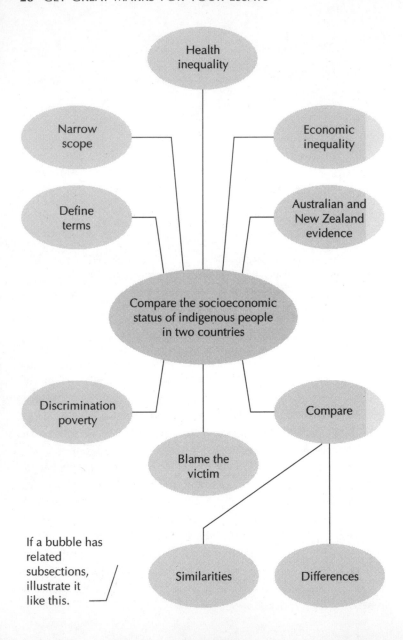

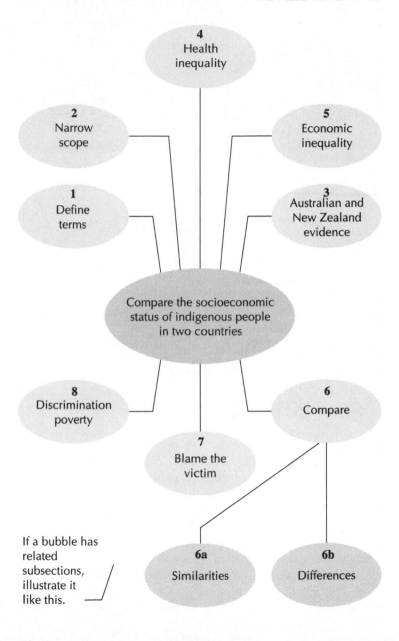

Mindmapping.

STAGE 3: DEVELOPING YOUR ARGUMENT

Most essay questions ask you to take a stance: do you agree or disagree? Which theory best explains the evidence? The stance that you take is called your argument or sometimes it is referred to as the theme of the essay. Whatever approach you take, you may modify your theme or argument as you do more reading. It may even be acceptable not to take sides, but to evaluate the strengths and weaknesses in the various debates you cover. However, the approach you have taken in answering the question must be clear from your introduction onwards. Otherwise, the reader of your essay may be confused as to what you are trying to prove or argue. There is more on developing an argument in Chapter 4.

Handy hint: some essential investments

There are three essential investments you should make:
1. an Australian dictionary
2. a thesaurus
3. a discipline dictionary or a style guide.

An Australian dictionary will ensure you use the correct spelling and right words in your essays. American and British dictionaries sometimes contain words and phrases which are spelt differently and may also have different meanings than they do in Australia.

A thesaurus is a dictionary of similar words. It is especially useful in writing essays to help you use a greater variety of words. As often happens, when we write we tend to use the same word over and over again. A thesaurus provides you with alternatives which makes your writing more interesting to read. It is also helpful in those situations when a word is 'on the tip of your tongue' and you just can't think of the right word. Note that most computers come with an in-built dictionary and thesaurus, but check that they use Australian spelling.

Most disciplines either have specific dictionaries or style guides such as the *Publication Manual of the American Psychological Association*. Discipline dictionaries provide the specific meaning of terms used in a particular discipline, which can vary considerably from their literal meaning in everyday usage. Style guides provide information on how to write and reference your material for a particular discipline. They are often used in the science-based disciplines to provide consistent guidelines for authors in the field.

4

The art of analysis

What is the difference between being descriptive and being analytical? How do you do analysis in an essay? Why do you have to use theories and where does your opinion come in to it? By the end of this chapter you will find the answers to these questions.

Suspicion is a key factor in being an academic detective. In your search for facts, motives and explanations it is crucial that you be cautious and question the validity and credibility of the information your investigation of the essay topic turns up. 'There are many stories in the big city . . .' and your job is to determine which stories are believable and which ones have loopholes. Your suspicious nature is actually the basis of being analytical. With your detective's magnifying glass still in hand, this chapter will let you wade through the basic features of analysis as they will appear in your essays.

WHAT'S THIS THING CALLED ANALYSIS?

When you investigate an essay topic, you can divide your information into two parts: description and analysis. Let's use the example of building a house from toy building blocks. You use building blocks to make the toy house which is a single, whole object. So a whole essay topic is made up of interrelated parts. The descriptive part of the essay is the foundation. The mortar which holds the descriptive parts together is the analysis. To analyse a topic is to break it up into its various parts, the individual building blocks, to understand what each part means and to explain how the parts link together to form the whole. Being analytical in your essays means taking an essay topic apart block by block, until you are able to explain why things are the way they are. All essays need their descriptive parts, but it is the analysis which holds the parts together in order to answer the essay question.

BEING CRITICAL: KNOWING THE RIGHT QUESTION TO ASK . . .

Lord Byron said that 'knowing the right question to ask is half the answer'. This saying may sound a little silly at first, but knowing the right questions to ask is really what analysis is all about. The tertiary essay has to do more than simply describe a topic: it is not just a summary of your reading. Tertiary essays are about evaluating your material and determining the strengths and weaknesses of the evidence and theories you come across. You might ask yourself how, as a student, you could know these things. To be aware of what evidence and theories exist you need to read widely. Once you have an overview of the topic, you can start evaluating your material so that you can make conclusions and answer the essay question.

Being critical does not mean criticising for the sake of criticising things. In academic work, being critical means an objective assessment of the strengths and weaknesses of the theories and research findings involved. The best way to do analysis is to constantly keep in your mind the question, *Why*? Questioning why something is the way it is requires an answer. Sometimes such an approach is called *critical analysis*. In practice there is really not much difference between the terms 'analysis' and 'critical analysis'. 'Critical' is sometimes added to the term 'analysis' because it emphasises that you should be critical; that is, that you should question why things are the way they are and how they could be otherwise. Critical analysis is about seeking out alternative views and possible solutions to problems. You can only seriously do this by using a number of sources and reading with a 'critical', questioning mind. For example:

- How much confidence do you have in a particular study you have just read about?
- What aspects of the research bothered or impressed you?
- Do other studies come to different conclusions?

Continually ask yourself how each study, theory, fact, concept, definition or criticism fits in with what you know about the topic. If you do this, you are *doing* analysis. The example below briefly compares a descriptive part of an essay with an analytical part of an essay.

Example: Comparing description and analysis in an essay

Essay topic Is everyone —————— *The question needs to be*
equal in Australia? *answered by using*
descriptive evidence of
inequality and analysed
using various explanations
of why inequality exists.

There is clear evidence of
inequality in Australia. For
example, Aboriginal people *A descriptive section of*
have a life expectancy of *the essay which uses*
fifteen to twenty years less *evidence to make an*
that white people. *argument.*

Various theories attempt to
explain inequality . . .
Conservative theories ——————— *Description is always*
blame the victim and *necessary in an essay.*
ignore issues such as *However, what needs to*
discrimination and *follow is some analysis*
generations of poverty. *to answer why such*
Such theories argue that *inequality exists.*
Aboriginal people are
either intellectually or
culturally inferior despite
the lack of evidence to
support such views. Other
theories state that various *You need to analyse the*
forms of racism lie at the *strengths and weaknesses*
heart of providing the *of the theories you use*
answers to Aboriginal *as well.*
inequality.

Beware commonsense

Commonsense is not as common as you might think. It's
not uncommon for students to wonder why we need
theories at all and ask whether it's not all just a matter of
commonsense. Beware this temptation. Once upon a time
it was considered commonsense to believe the earth was
flat and the centre of the universe! Commonsense will vary
over time, between cultures and between people who have
different experiences. The motto of the academic detective
is to maintain what the twentieth century philosopher,
Bertrand Russell, called 'the constant need for constructive
doubt'. So before you can believe in something, you need
to maintain 'constructive doubt' and investigate differing
points of view and not suppress or ignore contradictory
information or alternative views. Remember, the academic
detective is always suspicious and takes nothing for granted

or on blind faith. If you have an opinion on a topic, you should be able to give reasons why you hold that opinion. You should also be aware of alternative views and address the issues presented by such perspectives.

WHY THEORIES?

Theories are used by authors to explain certain events based on researched evidence. A theory is a system of ideas which attempts to explain something. You will come across many theories in your reading for an essay topic. It is up to you to analyse how well theories fit the evidence. You may find it frustrating that there are so many competing and opposing theories on the same issue. Whilst we would all like to believe the world is based on simple facts, things are rarely black and white when dealing with humans, societies, politics and power. Facts can easily be distorted. Theories help to unmask and uncover reasons which are not obvious from a simple look at the facts.

You will notice that theories may even directly contradict each other. This can occur due to biases of the authors, the time period in which they were written or because of the philosophical assumptions on which the theories are grounded. When you apply the theories of other authors to your essay topic, you need not only to describe them, but to analyse them in terms of their strengths and weaknesses.

ARGUING YOUR CASE

Since there are different views and theories about why things are the way they are, it is important to be argumentative in your essays. This has nothing to do with losing your temper, but everything to do with addressing the range of differing opinion on a topic. If you only include one theory, you produce a one-sided essay which simply ignores any contradictory evidence or argument.

Since our knowledge changes over time, the evidence upon which theories are based changes and so do theories. Theories are constantly re-evaluated, modified or rejected over time.

I'm right/you're wrong. Convince me!

To get good essay marks it is important to develop a clear argument in your essay. The argument is your approach to answering the question or discussing an essay topic. An argument is a set of propositions which are supported by evidence and allow logical conclusions to be made. For example, if you were to do an essay on whether social class exists in Australia, your argument would be why you believed 'yes', 'no' or 'maybe'. After doing your research and evaluating the various theories and evidence, you might argue that:

I'm right, you're wrong!

(a) Australia is a classless society for the reasons you outline in your essay;

(b) Australia is a class based society; or

(c) there is evidence of inequality, but that class may not be as important as other factors such as gender or race.

Whatever your argument would be, you would have to canvass the other views and show why your view is more credible than the others.

Where does my opinion come into it?

Essays are meant to be an objective analysis of a particular topic. Your opinion plays a part in your interpretation of the topic in deciding what material is relevant and how it is organised and analysed, and in the construction of the argument. Your opinion comes into an essay when you are asked to evaluate the strengths and weaknesses of various arguments and make conclusions. The stance you take is your opinion. However, you do this by using *supporting evidence* that you gather in the research stage.

All well argued essays are able to support their argument with evidence; and to examine alternative explanations and the criticisms they make of the author's argument.

MY OPINION VERSUS INFORMED OPINION

An essay is an act of persuasion. The job of an academic detective is to convince others of what you have to say. You do this by using supporting evidence from an independent source, since this gives your argument credibility.

It is in my head, I know it's true, why can't I use it?

You *cannot* use an opinion or fact from your memory or experience unless you can find evidence to support it. If you use unsupported evidence your essay becomes unconvincing. For example, if you argue:

I know my opinion is right

someone could come along and simply say:

I disagree. I think you're wrong. Prove it.

We now have a stalemate! One opinion versus another.

If you have an opinion, you must support it with a credible and reliable source of evidence which can easily be checked. Otherwise, arguments or disagreements will never get any further than the above example. Academic study requires you to research supporting evidence. Remember, it is one thing to be opinionated, another to support your informed opinion with evidence.

SUPPORTING EVIDENCE: THE GOOD, THE BAD AND THE UGLY

There are three forms of supporting evidence.

The good. That which is relevant to your topic, provides enough detail to support what you are saying and is properly referenced from a credible source.

The bad. Where the evidence is overly vague, not related to your argument and not referenced to a credible source.

The ugly. A biased representation of the evidence due to presenting one side of the argument and ignoring alternative sources of information. Take a look at the example below which contains a statement from a student's essay.

Example: Sloppy detective work

Everyone is equal. Everyone has the opportunity to work hard and succeed. People who are rich have worked hard for their success. In Australia, everyone has an equal chance of being successful.

These are unsupported statements which lack credibility. They are based on sloppy detective work. An academic detective would ask for the evidence and the source. Otherwise such statements are just opinionated nonsense. As an academic detective your suspicious nature makes you look for alternative views and evidence. Being critical and holding such statements up to scrutiny by good detective work is what analysis based on supporting evidence is all about.

The lecture said it all, why can't I just use that?

By all means use your lecture notes to help you understand a topic or as a starting point to guide your research, but

The lecturer said it.

in general, do not reference your lecture notes. Always try to find the information you have been given in a lecture from a written source, such as a book or article. Your lecture notes are not a reliable or credible source of information. It is impossible to prove that you correctly understood and copied down information delivered in a lecture.

If you need to find the source of what was said in a lecture, most lecturers provide a reference list to the material they have used in a lecture, or will do so upon request. However, in some cases a lecturer may provide original material in a lecture that cannot be obtained from another source. If this applies to the information you want to use, it is permissible to reference the lecture.

'Wisest is she who knows she does not know.'

Jostein Gaarder in the novel *Sophie's World* came up with this saying to highlight that wisdom is not about how much you know. It is about accepting that you cannot know everything and that there may be things which contradict and challenge what you believe. In forming an argument and analysing an essay topic, it is important to keep an open mind, to maintain constructive doubt.

There are very few simple answers to the various essay topics you are likely to encounter. Always strive to find the evidence for your argument and evaluate the opposing theories so that you avoid being biased. Bias refers to prejudices and preconceptions which distort your ability to assess information in an impartial manner. Bias can arise when you believe a certain thing irrespective of whether there is evidence to support it. To avoid bias ensure you **do not**:

- present a one-sided argument by relying on one author, theory or text
- suppress or ignore contradictory information and alternative views.

ANALYSIS AS ART

Doing analysis is an art form. It is only possible to learn analysis by actually attempting to do it. The art of analysis can be likened to that of the painter who studies the subject to be painted and does many sketches before paint is committed to canvas. The academic detective needs a magnifying glass to sift through the clues that rise from his or her reading, just as the painter adds another layer to the canvas to alter the perspective of the subject being portrayed.

Throughout your reading for an essay topic you will come across conflicting perspectives or theories which attempt to explain the evidence. How well you analyse these different theories and the descriptive evidence you have dug up is truly a form of art. Happy painting; but remember, the *Mona Lisa* wasn't painted in a day!

The art of analysis.

5

Muckraking: how to find what you need

This chapter shows you how to find relevant information in an efficient way. It also gives you some hints on how to read academic material quickly and effectively.

An academic detective leaves no stone unturned searching for clues by using a variety of sources. Finding information is the muckraking phase of essay writing. You often have to wade through a lot of muck before you find understandable, recent and relevant information. Along the way, you may encounter a number of myths.

DEBUNKING MYTHS

There are a number of student myths about researching an essay which go around each year. They have little substance, but reflect the confusion of some students in not knowing how to find and use information.

Myth 1: the one answer to your prayers. Don't waste time looking for the elusive pot of information gold at the end of the rainbow; there is no single book or journal article which will magically provide all the material and

There must be an easy way.

answers for your essay question. You are meant to use a variety of sources of information to ensure you have covered the field and found the relevant information. Even supposedly neutral introductory textbooks should be treated with caution. There will be parts which are more detailed, clearer or better written than others. It is for this reason that you should consult a number of sources.

Myth 2: there is no information on my topic. Another falsehood often quoted by students is that they just cannot find any information on their topic. The truth is they either have not looked hard enough, or have not looked in the right place. This chapter will help to show how to find what you need.

Myth 3: there is too much information. One other excuse used is that there are just too many publications on a topic, making it impossible for you to select or summarise the appropriate information within the given word limit. This is no excuse. You are meant to try. The marker realises that many books have been written on particular topics; you are not meant to reproduce them in 2000 or 3000 words. The skill lies in selecting the important information and summarising it concisely in the given word limit. This is where you earn your marks.

Myth 4: there must be an easy way. A final myth is that there is an easy way to do research. Forget it. Whilst computers and information technology have certainly sped things up, finding information is still about muckraking. You need to wade through all the muck out there to find the good stuff. This chapter gives you some pointers about time-saving ways of finding what you need.

WHERE TO START LOOKING FOR INFORMATION

Confused? You are not alone. The key places to start looking for information are:
- lecture notes
- your textbook
- introductory texts
- discipline dictionaries
- subject reference lists
- bibliographies
- key word searches using CD-Rom databases.

Using your lecture notes

Lecture notes are a good starting point as they identify key authors, theories and concepts. These can be used to help narrow down your search for information. Lecture notes should be used as a guide only. Do not rewrite your lecture notes straight into your essay. There is nothing academics like less than reading their own lectures in student essays.

Confused? You are not alone.

Your textbook

If your textbook covers the essay topic, your lecturer/tutor will normally expect you to use it and refer to it. It is surprising how many students ignore the relevant parts of their textbook when looking for information.

Introductory texts

Introductory texts are easy to read and present summaries of topics. Find the introductory books for your subject and scan the content and index pages for relevant material, using the key words and issues you uncovered by brainstorming (see Chapter 3). Introductory books summarise the literature in plain terms and give you an idea of the range of research and explanations on your particular topic. Do not just stop at one introductory book; look at a few as the coverage varies. Even if you end up not using them in your essay, introductory books can help to clarify what you should be looking for.

Discipline dictionaries

Most disciplines have specialised dictionaries such as for economics, environmental studies, biology, nursing, law and anthropology. These are invaluable for clarifying concepts and theories. Dictionaries provide brief summaries of concepts, theories and theorists. They often give references to other related entries in the dictionary and for further reading. If you intend to major in a particular discipline, it is advisable to purchase a copy of the relevant dictionary. However, most libraries will have copies.

Reading lists

Some lecturers will provide a reading list to guide your research and they may even place some of the material in your library on reserve or short loan. If your lecturer or tutor has gone to the trouble of doing so, it is probably advisable to look at what's on offer. Whilst there may be many books on a reading list, remember that you are not expected to read whole books; often only a chapter or even a few pages may be relevant to your essay. Use the content and index pages to help find what you need. **Caution:** Reading lists are not exhaustive and you may find better and more up to date information which is not on the reading list. By all means consult the lists, but do not rely solely on them.

Bibliographies: the springboard technique

A good way to find more information on a topic is to use the books used by other authors. Once you find a couple of books or articles, have a look at their bibliography or reference lists. In this way you can see which books or articles the authors have consulted, and you can look up these references yourself.

Of course, not all the references used by authors you read will be relevant. If you come across a section in a book or article which is relevant to your essay, note which authors are referenced and find them in the bibliography. Check the dates to see when they were written and look at the titles and place of publication. If these are relevant, then look them up yourself.

Key word searches

Once you have started your research your textbook, discipline dictionary and introductory books should give you a good idea of the key writers, ideas and theories your essay has to cover. These act as signposts or key words when you search for more information. Think of the key words around a particular topic or concept and plug them into your library computer or CD-Rom database. For example, if you were looking for information on obesity, you could search for the terms 'obesity', 'overweight', 'fat', 'diet', 'food', 'body shape/size/image'. You could even widen your search to include books on health and check their contents and index pages.

HOW TO FIND THE MATERIAL YOU NEED

Get to know your library well. At the start of your course, take a library tour or ask a librarian to show you what the library has to offer. Libraries have printed information in the form of booklets or 'flyers' on the services they offer. Most libraries organise their material using the Dewey decimal classification system. This means that no matter which library you are in, books will be catalogued in the same way and be given a similar catalogue number. For example, under the Dewey system philosophy books have 'call numbers' between 100 and 199. Language call numbers range between 400 and 499, and literature call numbers range between 800 and 899. Geography starts at 910, law at 340, architecture at 710 and medicine at 610.

Therefore, it is a good idea to learn which call numbers your discipline is catalogued under since often the best way to find books is by browsing the relevant shelves in the library.

The first thing to do when you have found a relevant book or article is to find out:

- *when* it was published to see if it is up to date
- *where* it was published.

It is easy to overlook this and end up using out-of-date material or information which applies to another country. For example, it is useless to provide the unemployment rate for 1985 if you are discussing current rates of unemployment. Be careful when you use overseas publications for relevant theories and research findings and remember to note when and where they were written. If you forget to do this, you could mistakenly apply information about another country to your own.

Finding journals: information technology at your fingertips

Journals are important sources of information because they provide more up-to-date research and detailed evidence on specific topics than many books. Most libraries keep the latest issue of a journal in a display section until the next issue arrives, and allow the display issue only to be read (but not borrowed) until it is superseded by the next issue. Usually only staff are allowed to borrow journals. Note that when you go searching for a journal, it may still be on the display shelves or may have already been borrowed by staff. The issue you are looking for may also be in the process of being bound. Most journals are bound every year into an annual volume. Check with library staff if the journal appears to be missing from the shelf and they will inform you if it is being bound and when it will be available.

In days gone by, to find a journal article you would manually have to plough through volumes of indices such as the *Sociological Abstracts* or APAIS (Australian and Public Affairs Information Service). These indices contain all the abstracts (or summaries) of journal articles published in the discipline. The indices list all journal articles by topic, author and key words. They are updated regularly. The number of journals varies with the index, ranging from a couple of hundred to the thousands. Whilst most libraries will have the hard copy version of the indices, all journal information is now accessible via computer on CD-Rom. This makes the whole process of finding journal articles quick and easy.

CD-Rom databases

'CD' stands for 'compact disc' and 'Rom' stands for 'read only memory', meaning that the CDs can be read but not recorded on. A CD-Rom is just like a music CD, but instead contains visual information, usually in the form of written text. Multimedia CD-Roms are the latest version and combine sound, text and pictures. Most libraries have CD-Roms on just about every discipline, covering almost every journal imaginable.

It is important for you to become familiar with using CD-Roms. Using IT (information technology), as it is often referred to, is an important skill and one which can add to your employability. Being able to use CD-Roms will not only help your present education, but also your continuing education, since many workplaces now subscribe to relevant databases. Not too far into the future, anyone with a computer in their house will be able to access such information via the 'phone line. You can search CD-Rom databases by either typing in an author, title or word/topic. Libraries often publish their own handouts on how to use the databases. Thankfully most of them are fairly similar and intuitive—that is, they use menus which are easy to follow. A list of some of the many CD-Rom databases is provided below. There are many more databases in existence so check your library holdings.

Using newspapers

Newspapers can be an important source of current information. However, they should be treated with caution. There are often many errors in our newspapers. There is also bias and little analysis of the issues, so do not base an important fact or argument on information sourced from a newspaper. By all means use information from newspapers to add to your case or provide examples, but ensure that you have more credible, academic sources of information as well.

Handy hint: CD-Rom databases

AUSLIT Over 140 000 citations to books, journals, film, video and newspapers on Australian literature.

AUSTROM Social science, humanities, politics, sport, home economics, criminology and law. It includes **APAIS** (Australian and Public Affairs Information Service) which collates journal and newspaper articles on Australian political, economic, social, legal and cultural affairs.

BUSINESS AUST. Business, tax and industrial relations issues.

CELIS Conservation and the environment.

CINAH International: nursing, allied health and consumer health literature.

CURRENT CONTENTS International: contents pages of over 20 000 journals on all subjects.

ECONLIT International: economics, public finance, management, labour and law.

ERIC International education journals.

HISTORICAL ABSTRACT World historical literature from 1450 to the present.

HUMANITIES INDEX Classical studies, history, language, literature, religion, performing arts.

LAWPAC Australian case law (High Court and Federal Court decisions).

MEDLINE International, with over 3000 medical and biological journals.

PHILOSOPHER'S INDEX Over 270 journal abstracts on related fields to philosophy.

PSYCHLIT International: psychology, psychiatry, related health and legal matters.

SOCIOFILE International: sociology and anthropology.

UNCOVER International, with over 40 000 journals from all fields.

Vital statistics

Many countries have government agencies which compile statistics. For example, the Australian Bureau of Statistics (ABS) compiles a whole range of statistics on Australia. It regularly publishes Census data and information compiled from specific surveys. The areas are too numerous to mention, but most libraries will carry a significant amount of ABS material. Increasingly the ABS is becoming more user-friendly and is publishing specialist documents and books on selected topics such as the status of women, Aboriginal people and general social indicators. These are extremely useful sources of information.

Governments also publish many useful documents through their various departments. You can contact the department you are interested in and ask for a publication brochure (such as the Department of Industrial Relations). Sometimes independent bodies are established by the government to compile information and undertake research on specific topics. In Australia, an example in the health and welfare field is the AIHW (Australian Institute of Health and Welfare) which produces many helpful publications. International comparisons of data are usually found in OECD (Organisation for Economic Co-operation and Development) and World Bank publications. Many of these publications are available in libraries or through book shops.

6

Making sense of all the information you gather

This chapter outlines how to make effective notes from your reading which will save you time by producing organised notes. You need to do this after you have found information relevant to your essay topic and before you begin to write your essay.

Once you have found a number of sources of information, what do you do with it? A major benefit of using a number of sources is that you will find that some writers provide greater detail and are more interesting and understandable than others. When you search for material on a topic, don't worry if some of the material you find repeats itself. Re-reading similar information written by a different author helps to reinforce your understanding. Remember to read with a purpose; keep the essay topic and your essay plan in mind. Refer to your essay plan and be familiar with key words, concepts and theories.

HOW TO READ AN ACADEMIC BOOK

Reading an academic book takes concentration. It's easy to get frustrated when you initially find a book difficult to understand at the first sitting. Reading an academic book is not like flipping through a magazine or even a work of fiction. Academic books take more time and effort. In some cases you may need to read a section of an article or book a number of times. To help clear your mind and focus your concentration, see Chapter 7 for more applications of the mindmapping technique.

For intensive reading, read section by section or a few pages at a time. Read each section a few times over and make notes. If you are still finding the information difficult to understand, find other sources on the same topic. Go back to introductory books and then return to your original source for another try. However, do not discount the fact that what you are reading may be poorly written. Just because it is published does not mean it is well written. Remember this yourself in your own writing; long-winded sentences packed with big words do not make good writing or good reading. Look around for more clearly written pieces on the same topic by other authors.

FINDING RELEVANT INFORMATION: LET'S GO SKIMMING

If you feel you have too many books and articles, there is a quick way to determine if they are useful. The quick reading or scanning technique is called 'skimming'. It is not meant to replace actual reading, but should be used to filter what information is relevant to your essay. When you have found a book which seems to be relevant, use the table of contents and the index to find the relevant sections. With journal articles, read the abstract, introduction and conclusion and skim the subheadings. For skimming books, see the 'Handy hint' box below.

Let's go skimming.

Handy hint: how to skim a book

1. Turn to the table of contents and the index to find the relevant parts.
2. First read only the introduction and conclusion of a chapter as this will give you a good idea of what the author is saying.
3. If it looks promising, simply read the first and last sentences of each paragraph (the topic and linking sentences).

Remember it is not necessary to read or use a whole chapter or book. Only certain sections will be relevant to your needs.

WARNING: skimming is a method to help you find relevant material quickly. It is not a substitute for detailed reading and analysis of that material.

TAKING NOTES

Once you start detailed reading, it is time to take notes. How you go about taking notes is up to you. Different people will use different methods. The most common and effective method is *the filing system* which can be used on paper or with a computer. The main advantage of this method of note taking is that it keeps all related material together, so you do not have to search through all of your notes to find a point you vaguely remember noting somewhere! The filing system has three easy steps.

Step 1. Use a computer or piece of paper and place a heading on the page indicating a key term, concept or theory. Repeat this for all the basic parts of your essay which you identified in your essay plan. In effect, what you are doing is making sub-plans of your essay, broken up into the various points you will cover. This is especially useful if your essay involves a complex or lengthy topic.

Sub-plans are particularly helpful when explaining and applying theories. Since theories can be complex and confusing at first, it may be better to break down your theory content in the form of a sub-plan. Are key words defined and referenced? Is there enough detail explaining the key aspects of the theory? What evidence exists to support or contradict the theory? What criticisms of the theory are made by other authors? What alternative theories exist? By mapping out these sorts of questions, you not only clarify these issues to yourself, but ensure your essay content is relevant and logically expressed. The diagram on page 58 provides an example of the filing system of note taking.

Step 2. On another sheet of paper or page on your computer, put the heading 'bibliography' or 'references'. As you take notes, write down the details of each book and article you use and give it a number. Then when you record your notes in each section, simply refer to the source by the number you gave it. This saves you rummaging through your notes trying to find the details of a particular book or article. Be sure to keep your reference list in a safe place. Instead of using a numbering system, an alternative is to write the full reference of each book or article you use on the page on which you take your notes.

When taking notes, you must record where you found the information. In academic essays you need to acknowledge your information; this is called referencing. Referencing means accurately noting the relevant bibliographic details of each source you use: names, titles, places and years of publications, publishers, editions, names of journals, volume numbers and page numbers. The 'how and why' of referencing is explained in Chapter 10.

Step 3. As you take notes, enter them on the topic headed pages. This way you immediately organise your notes into topics related to your essay. Grouping your notes in this way makes it easier to cut and paste various bits of information as you begin to draft your essay. Automatically organising your notes into distinct sections makes it easier to decide on the order of your material.

Alternatively, you can write up the notes of each section individually and then place them in essay order.

Beware the highlight trap

Some people like to photocopy pages and highlight as they read, perhaps making brief notes in the margin. You can use highlighting as long as this is not where your note taking ends. Sometimes you end up with most of the page coloured by a highlighter! Avoid trying to write your first essay draft from highlighted notes. You must take written notes because just highlighting parts of a photocopy from an article or book is not enough. By summarising the relevant parts of what you have read you begin to understand and remember the material. In addition, summarising your material in your own words actually saves you time, since once you put the information in your own words you don't waste time working out the meaning of a passage you have highlighted, every time you re-read it.

A final word of caution about highlighting is that if you copy highlighted information you may forget it was a direct quote and fail to acknowledge it, therefore falling into the plagiarism trap (for more information on plagiarism see Chapter 10).

Example: Note taking

The topic headings are an easy way for you to organise your notes automatically as you take them. Some headings may be discarded, revised, added or deleted as more reading is done and notes are taken.

> **CLASS**
>
> *Ref 2*
> *page 5:*
> Karl Marx argues:
> "the ideas of the ruling
> class are in every epoch
> the ruling ideas"

Note that the direct quote has been clearly identified in the notes by using quotation marks

> **GENDER**
>
> *Ref 1*
> *page 23:*
> the sexual division of
> labour represents the
> way in which various
> jobs, tasks and roles in
> society are divided
> between men and women

The numbers (e.g. Ref 1) correspond to the reference list on a separate page containing all the bibliographic details (such as author, date, publisher . . .)

ETHNICITY

Ref 3
pages 123–124:
there is no such thing as
an 'ethnic'. It is derogatory
and assumes all people of
an ethnic origin are the
same. Many members of
ethnic groups in Australia
have significantly different
cultures, religions

Paraphrased
information (in
your own words)
should still be
clearly identified
by page number
and source of
information

Taking notes.

Paraphrasing

As mentioned above, most of the notes you take should be paraphrased—that is, you should summarise the relevant information from your reading *in your own words*. Do not simply copy slabs, 'word for word', from books or articles you read. This is time-consuming and you may later find it difficult to write your essay in your own words. Summarise in your own words what you have read after finishing a section of a chapter or article (see the paraphrased information in the previous example).

Direct quotes

Direct quotes can be used in essays to emphasise a particular point or to provide an example of another author's perspective or theory. If you actually write down a direct quote (word for word from the author) in your notes, ensure that you have recorded the passage exactly as you found it. Identify the direct quote in your notes by quotation marks. Record the page number of the source. It is important you do this in your notes so that you avoid losing marks for not showing direct quotes because of sloppy note taking.

How many notes?

It is difficult to answer this often-asked question; the number of notes will depend on the topic, the nature of the question and the word limit. A rule of thumb is to aim for double the word limit. So for an essay of 2000 words, or around 10 pages, you should have 20 pages of notes. You should not have fewer notes than the required essay word limit. In other words, do not try to expand your notes to fit the essay length; this just results in padding the essay out, or what essay markers refer to as 'waffle' (see Chapter 8). Too few notes mean you are forced to make generalisations with little proof or detail, and your essay will be unconvincing because there is no evidence to support the statements you make. On the other hand, if you have too many notes, your essay may be confused and unclear because you have been unable to clearly arrange your information, and you may find it difficult to stick to the word limit.

Too many/too few notes.

7

Doing essay drafts

How do you overcome writer's block? What's the best way to start writing an essay? This chapter shows you how to translate your notes into your first essay drafts. It shows you how to overcome writer's block with mindmapping, how to deal with word limits and ends with an essay content checklist.

Have you ever wondered why it is that just when you need to think of a 'perfect' opening sentence, you think about what you're going to have for dinner! Or you remember the friend you were supposed to call . . . or one of a million little things which seem to distract you from writing that perfect opening line. Though it can be very frustrating to your creative process, it is no surprise that such thoughts pop into your head. You've probably been busy all day and this is the first time you've sat down amidst some peace and quiet. Since you have some time to think and reflect, your brain takes the opportunity to remind you of all these important matters. They are important, but that doesn't help you to get started on your essay.

Overcoming writer's block.

STUCK FOR WORDS: OVERCOMING WRITER'S BLOCK

Most authors will tell you the trick to overcoming writer's block is to write something each day even if you feel it is not your best effort. However, mindmapping can help you to avoid staring at a blank page. We met the process of mindmapping back in Chapter 3, where it was helpful in planning an essay. Mindmapping is also an effective and rapid technique for dealing with writer's block by clearing the 'clutter' out of your mind.

What's on your mind? . . . how to use mindmapping to clear your mind

Here's how mindmapping can help. Once again, start with an idea in a bubble in the centre of a blank page.

MIND CLUTTER

Then you simply write down all the unwanted thoughts in your head as they flow out. Write down whatever you are thinking or comes to mind.

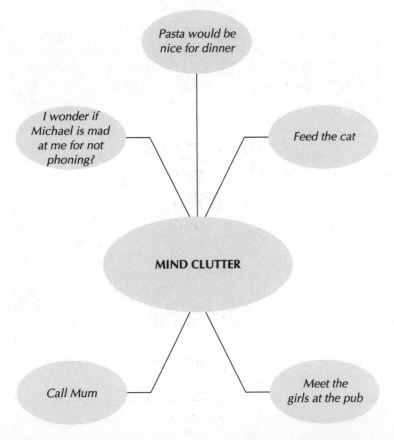

Once all of these thoughts are down on paper you can trust that they will not disappear and therefore they can be dismissed from your conscious mind. This leaves room for you to focus on your essay. Keep your mindmap close by, just in case any more stray thoughts pop into your head that you might need to add. Once you have set aside these thoughts, refer to your essay plan and your notes to start the creative process.

Handy hint: mindmap applications

Mindmapping to clear your mind of clutter is also a useful technique to help you focus your attention in lectures and exams or to help you concentrate when reading. It also helps you to get back to sleep at 4 a.m. when your mind seems to be inundated with thoughts!

Mind clutter.

TO CREATE AND EDIT

First of all you need to reject the thought that you can write the perfect sentence the first time you set out to write up your essay from your notes. Most people who do well at essays spend time planning, drafting and revising their writing. The important point to remember is to separate the writing process into two parts: the *creative* process and the *editing* process.

There is a distinct difference between creating and editing your writing. The creative part of writing is when you begin to put words together from your notes; you create the sentences. The editing process starts when you have finished writing and you begin to fix up your sentence structure and expression. You will make the writing process harder for yourself if you try to create and edit at the same time. If every time you begin to write, you stop to edit the sentence you just wrote, you interrupt the creative juices and end up with very little on paper.

ATMOSPHERE: SETTING THE SCENE

It is important for you to find a place to write where you feel physically and emotionally comfortable. Where this place is really depends on your personality. Some students can work only in libraries, free from home distractions, whilst others find public places too distracting and prefer the solitude of home. When you find such a place, try always to do your writing there since your mind will associate that place with writing and concentration.

The best atmosphere is one free of distractions. This means making sure that you have all the necessary equipment: pens, papers, notes and books in the one place. By all means have food and drink handy. Some people find music a good way to block out all other distractions, others just find it a distraction. The key to getting the atmosphere right is to ensure that interruptions from friends, partners

Making the mood.

and family are kept to a minimum. Schedule some time for reading, note taking, writing and general studying, and let people know that you will be *incommunicado* for that particular time.

ACTION PLAN: THE FIRST DRAFT

The first draft of the essay is your attempt to put your organised notes into an essay format. By this stage you should have sorted, selected, rejected and ordered the various parts of your notes. In the first draft, do not concern yourself with spelling, punctuation, expression or topic sentences; leave them for the following drafts. For now your objective is to get something down on paper. It is time for the creative process in which you translate your notes, ideas and essay plan into sentences and paragraphs.

Pause and review

Try not to do the whole essay, from first to final draft, in one sitting. When the first draft is complete, take a break. It often helps to distance yourself from your essay drafts for a few days if you can spare the time. By distancing yourself from your essay you are likely to be more objective about what you have written and better able to determine whether you are on track. Go back to your essay plan and compare it with your first draft. Check whether you have covered the areas that you intended to cover in the plan.

THE IMPASSE: TIME TO SEEK HELP

You may reach a stage in the essay draft process when you feel like you have hit a brick wall. Mindclearing or simply giving yourself a break from the essay can help. However, if you are still having problems there are three things you can do:
1. Talk it out loud.
2. Revise your plan.
3. See your tutor.

Talk it out loud and make sure what's in your head gets to paper

A good way to check if you understand what you are writing about is to explain it to someone else. Talk over issues with a classmate, friend or family member. Explain what you are trying to say in your essay. By talking out loud, you will quickly see whether you have a grasp of the topic. More often than not, what usually happens is that you are better able to express your essay content verbally than in written form. It's not unusual to have a good understanding of the topic in your head, but this fails to get translated to paper. So talking it out loud can help to clarify your understanding.

Revise your plan

Sometimes you may need to go back to your essay plan and revise it. This happens when your essay has gone off track from the original plan, or you uncover other new issues and information that need to be included during the draft writing process. Revising your plan may mean a return to the muckraking phase of getting more information (see Chapter 5). Do not get flustered or disappointed with yourself if this happens. It is quite common to need to revise plans and go in search of more information.

Seek help

If you are at a writing impasse, it may be time to make an appointment to see your tutor and discuss your essay. This is not an admission of failure. Lecturers and tutors are there to help you. It is their job to offer advice, guidance and clarify issues for you. As a lecturer I am surprised at how few students make use of their lecturer or tutor when they are having essay troubles. Sometimes a simple 'phone call can help to clarify the issues enormously. So if you find yourself in this situation, don't be backward in coming forward. However, as discussed in Chapter 2, do not turn up to a meeting with your lecturer/tutor with a blank slate. Prepare a list of questions to make best use of the time.

DRAFTS 2 AND 3 AND . . . PLACE YOURSELF IN THE MARKER'S SHOES

The number of drafts you do is up to you, but three would be a minimum. It will clearly depend on the time you have to complete the assessment task as well as the amount of effort that is required for the task. During the second and third draft stages your essay should be taking shape. This is the time for you to work on your sentence and paragraph structure. If you need a reminder, go back to

Chapter 2 to see how to do this. Try to put yourself in the shoes of the marker. What will he or she be expecting? What mark would you give yourself?

WORD LIMITS: QUALITY, NOT QUANTITY

Part of the skill of writing is to cover a topic within a given word limit. If you write substantially below or beyond the limit, you may be penalised. A good guide is to stick to a hundred words either side of the limit (above or below). Some lecturers allow greater latitude, setting 10 per cent above or below the essay word target as acceptable, but it is always advisable to check.

If you write significantly below the word limit, it is likely you have not covered the topic in the depth required. If your work is substantially over the word limit, the most common response of the marker is to stop reading the essay once the word target has been exceeded and give a mark on the essay to that point. It is unfair to other students if a substantially longer essay is accepted, especially since some topics have whole books written on them.

The hardest cut of all

Once you have a draft of the essay you are happy with, it is fairly common to find you have exceeded the word limit. This is not a problem in itself. In fact, it is much better to have too many words than too few. The real problem is how to cut your own work. This is the hardest cut of all! The most straightforward method of determining what stays or goes, or what should be reduced in length, is to return to your plan. Often there is a lot of repetition in essay drafts due to the overlap of information from a number of sources. It is also common to have wordy expression which needs cutting. All authors find it difficult to cut their own work. Think about it; you've worked long and hard to write all those words. Giving yourself some time away from your essay helps to make the task of trimming it a lot easier. Remember to be critical of your own work; imagine you are the marker. Go through your essay line by line, sentence by sentence, paragraph by paragraph and see what can be cut and improved. Keep the following in mind:

- Short, concise sentences are always better than long ones. If you have a sentence that is three or four lines long you are probably trying to say too much in one sentence or have used wordy expression. Try to split it into two sentences which make sense on their own.

- Be direct in what you are trying to say. It is easy to fall into the trap of writing in generalities when a direct approach would be clearer and take up fewer words.

- It is difficult to write concise, but detailed, sentences. It takes time and practice. Part of the reason for having word limits for essays is to encourage you to be concise with your words (see Chapter 8 for hints on how to do this).

The hardest cut.

Handy hint: essay content checklist

- Does your introduction state what your argument will be and what your essay is about?
- Check your essay structure: go through each paragraph and check the topic and linking sentences. If you read the first 'topic' sentence of each paragraph, does a clear outline of your essay become apparent?
- Summarise each paragraph in one line (what is the paragraph saying?) and write each line below the other to form a flow chart of the essay content and argument. Does the flow chart make sense? Does it have a logical flow?
- Length: is your essay close to the word limit, that is, 100 words over or under the target?
- Have you answered the question? Compare the finished product with the plan (have you done what you said you would?). Be especially careful to check that you have covered all the aspects you imply in your introduction.
- Do you have supporting evidence for the claims you make?
- Is your content accurate, concise, detailed and specific?
- If asked to make an assessment, evaluation or give a specific answer, have you done so?
- Does your conclusion answer the question? Does it sum up your argument?

8

Easy marks: the unwritten rules of academic writing

The unwritten rules of academic writing, once learnt, are not forgotten. The rules are rarely spoken of, but without them your essays are likely to be penalised. The rules are simple to follow, and once you know them you will no longer lose 'easy' marks on your essay.

As you've seen throughout the earlier chapters of this book, to be a good academic detective you have to follow the rules of the essay game. You've planned, brainstormed, collected information and written your first essay drafts. However, you have a hunch that there is more to getting good marks than learning the rules and skills of essay writing. You are absolutely right! Essay writing is both a skill and an art form. The art of writing good essays is a creative process and is not taught, but learnt through experience and practice. However, this chapter and the next will give you some pointers about where marks are won and lost, which will help to improve the creative side of your writing.

The rude shock.

THE SKILL AND ART OF WRITING

Do you read other students' work or the academic books you consult and wonder why can't you write like that? When academics mark essays they take into account how well written an essay is and how sophisticated the expression of the student's ideas. It is often assumed that students have this 'art' of writing and when they do not, it is up to the student somehow to acquire it. In the end the way you construct sentences and how you express your thoughts is a creative process. Whilst most tertiary institutions now have centres established to help students with writing and studying, there is no replacement for practice. Once you know the rules of essay writing, you can usually guarantee that you will at least pass your essay since you would have developed the *skill* of writing. However, the *art* of writing takes longer to develop. The more essays you write, the more drafts you do and the more things you read, the sooner you will develop the art of writing.

THE RUDE SHOCK

It is not uncommon for students to get a rude shock when they get their first piece of work back and their mark is below what they expected. Sometimes this is because students are unclear about what markers want and the standard of work required. This section will help you to avoid the pitfalls in academic writing, giving you an idea of the writing standard required. When you write, be careful not to confuse the way you speak with the way you write. When we speak, we often use informal language, such as slang, emotion and imprecise statements. Academic writing must be clear, concise and objective. For the sake of accessibility, please note that this book has been written in a style less formal than that required of academic writing. Therefore, in essays, your writing style should not mimic this book, but instead should follow the 'unwritten rules of academic writing' as depicted in this chapter.

The following example will help to clarify what markers see as unacceptable and where you lose marks. Take a look at the 'What's wrong?' example below and see if you spot anything familiar. Test your detective powers and see how many mistakes you can find.

Exercise: What's wrong?

'Men and women are victims of their anatomy', in my opinion people are simply products of there culture. The process by which individuals learn a culture, socialisation involves learning social rules and expectations of behaviour that can be divided into two stages, i.e. primary and secondary socialisation. I believe that time, place, age, status & job, etc. can all effect values, attitudes and behaviour—the socialisation we all recieve—and may well affect the treatment we recieve as they're is no knowing the hell that a man goes through in that, their is only one thing that really matters and that is that there is adequate socialisation to prepare one for life. Its man that believes he controls his own destiny, but at the same time an individuals own personality is also shaped by the culture in which they live Meads theory is that this process is shaped by social interaction and occurs in three distinct stages of human developement.

The exercise is reproduced opposite, but this time with a marker's comments and corrections. Whilst the exercise represents an extreme case, the mistakes contained in the paragraph reflect the most common essay mistakes. If you can avoid the problems in the example, then easy marks will not be lost. For example, if an essay was out of 20 and a marker was to subtract half a mark for each mistake, there would be few marks left to actually give to the content of the essay. This may seem harsh, but a tertiary standard essay is expected to be professional and not be riddled with such basic mistakes. Many students lose easy marks because they fail to take the necessary precautions. The rest of this chapter is devoted to showing you how to take those precautions.

KEY FEATURES OF GOOD ACADEMIC WRITING

Students often complain that academics speak and write in an unnecessarily complex way. There will always be examples of academics who speak and write in a difficult way. However, most academic writing is not unnecessarily complex; it is just different from fiction or everyday speech. Academic writing is meant to be:

- formal, not personal
- without repetition or clichés
- active, not passive
- objective, not biased

Exercise: What's wrong? . . . the answers

'Men and women are victims of their anatomy', in my
    reference?
opinion people are simply products of (there) culture. The
    unnecessary   *spelling*
process by which individuals learn a culture, socialisation
    comma
involves learning social rules and expectations of behaviour

that can be divided into two stages, (i.e.) primary and
    avoid abbreviations   *define*
secondary socialisation. I believe that time, place, age, status
    define *spelling* *unnecessary*
(&) job, (etc.) can all effect values, attitudes and behaviour—the
    avoid abbreviations
socialisation we all (recieve)—and may affect the treatment
    spelling
we (recieve) as (they're) is no knowing the hell that a man goes
    spelling
through in that, (their) is only one thing that really matters and
    emotive, slang, waffle—needed a rewrite
that is that there is adequate socialisation to prepare one for
It's   *who*
life. (Its) (man) (that) believes (he) controls (his) own destiny, but at
    sexist
the same time an individu(als) own personality is also shaped
    apostrophe
by the culture in which they live Me(ads) theory is that this
    full stop   *apostrophe*
process is shaped by social interaction and occurs in three
    spelling   *reference*
distinct stages of human devel(ope)ment.
    What are the three stages?

- detailed and specific, not imprecise or vague
- devoid of slang or emotive expression.

Write—don't talk: keep it formal

It is natural to wish to write the way you speak. However, for tertiary essays it is necessary to write in an academic manner which differs from the way you speak. The more you read, the more you learn to write in a formal, academic way. To compare the difference between spoken and written language, see the 'What's wrong?' exercise below, reproduced once again, but this time how it should have been written in the first place.

Example: what's wrong is now right

'Men and women are victims of their anatomy' (Apple, 1990:12). People are products of their culture. The process by which individuals learn a culture, socialisation, involves learning social rules and expectations of behaviour that can be divided into two stages: primary and secondary socialisation. Primary socialisation represents the influences in early childhood from the family. Secondary socialisation reflects factors external to the family, such as friends, school and the media (Apple, 1995:5–7). Time, place, age, status and occupation can all affect the values, attitudes and behaviour—the socialisation we all receive (Apple, 1990:67–70).

Individuals generally believe they control their own destiny, but at the same time, an individual's own personality is shaped by the culture in which they live. Mead's (1945) theory is that this process is shaped by social interaction and occurs in three distinct stages of human development. The three stages are . . .

Avoid repetition and clichés

In the early drafts of your essay it is common to find parts which repeat themselves, either directly or by saying the same thing in a slightly different way. Repetition is a key feature of everyday speech. We often repeat ourselves for clarity, to reinforce a point or sometimes to simply fill the silence as we think of the next thing to say. As the following example shows: 'If you re-read your work, you may find on re-reading it that a lot of repetition can be found by the simple act of re-reading'!

Clichés are also common in everyday speech. Clichés are overused phrases which have specific meanings in a particular culture at a particular time. You can never be certain that people understand what they mean, so avoid clichés, for example, 'like the plague'! They tend to employ emotive imagery and can lead to misunderstanding, lack of accuracy and lack of objectivity. Read the excerpt from the *Yes, Prime Minister* series as a case of cliché overload. Just what does the character Desmond Gladesbrook actually say?

Example: avoiding clichés

The character Desmond Gladesbrook, explaining why he is against a government inquiry:

> You know, if you spill the beans you open up a whole can of worms. I mean, how can you let sleeping dogs lie if you let the cat out of the bag? You bring in a new broom and if you're not very careful you find you've thrown the baby out with the bath water. Change horses in the middle of a race, next thing you know you're up the creek without a paddle.

Active, not passive writing

Passive writing is wordy and dull. Active writing uses active verbs and gets to the point. Active sentences are structured

to start with the main point. Active writing avoids unnecessary words (that is, words which do not add any meaning
to the sentence) and reflects a direct style of writing. Such
a direct approach is different from the personal and
informal nature of everyday speech. For example, the
following sentences can be rewritten from the passive to
the active, making them shorter and clearer:

'The implementation of the outcomes of the policy
making process are intended to be undertaken within
the year', could easily be rewritten to, 'The policy will
be implemented by the end of the year'.

Another example: 'It was argued by Marx . . .' could
easily be changed to, 'Marx argued . . .'

In both examples, the writing is active and says the
same thing in a simpler, shorter and more direct way.

Padding it out: steer clear of waffle and verbosity

Waffle or verbose (wordy) writing is what academics call
the unnecessary use of complex or too many words.
Sometimes students try to artificially 'pad out' their essays
to meet the word limit, or they write complicated sentences
to make their essays sound more academic. It is easy to
fall into the trap of writing around a subject rather than
about the actual subject itself. Many students waste too
much essay space on continually stating what they intend
to do, rather than actually just getting to the point. It is
easy for markers to spot such 'padding'; all it does is
obscure what you are trying to say. A good warning sign
of padded writing is when your sentences are over 25
words long. When sentences are over two lines long, the
short term memory of your reader begins to wane. There
are times when a lengthy sentence is required, but check
to see if you can simplify the wording to shorten the
sentence. There is nothing inherently wrong with a long
sentence so long as it is well constructed but, in general,
shorter sentences are easier to read and understand.

Sometimes too many things are covered in the one sentence and are better broken up into two sentences. If a longer sentence or two shorter sentences say the same thing, then always use the shorter sentences. When writing the drafts of your essay, be critical of your use of words and sentences. Is your writing free of unnecessary words? The old saying is 'to make every word count', so look to see if you can use shorter sentences and simpler expression.

Handy hint: concise writing

Don't write: *Instead, write:*

- along the lines of   like
- at this point in time   now
- in terms of/in respect of   about/of
- makes the statement/observation   says/comments/
                                          states/observes

- in the event that   if
- due to/owing to the fact   since/because
- in order to/to be in the position to   to

'Right' words

There are a great variety of words in the English language. Whilst you should always try to write in a straightforward manner, this does not mean you cannot vary the types of words you use. Using a thesaurus can improve the clarity, specificity and sophistication of your writing. Also, try to use some variety in your sentence structure. Avoid starting each sentence with the same opening words. There is nothing more boring than reading an essay where every sentence begins with: 'It seems . . . It also seems . . . It seems . . . ' For some help with sentence structure, see the 'Handy hint' box below.

Handy hint: sentence starters

It can be seen that	The evidence is
Studies suggest	In addition
Furthermore	Therefore
However	Although
In conclusion/To sum up	Studies suggest
It would seem	It tends to be the case
As a result	Otherwise
Alternatively	For instance
Conversely	Consequently
Nevertheless	Nonetheless
Accordingly	Nevertheless
Nonetheless	Accordingly

Sentence starters.

Be accurate, precise and specific

Read the following example taken from a student essay discussing Aboriginal inequality:

'It is a well known fact that Aboriginal health is far worse, with high mortality and morbidity rates'.

There are a number of problems with the sentence. Firstly, is it really a well known fact? How *accurate* is this statement? Does this mean that there is plenty of evidence to prove that Aboriginal health is far worse, or does it mean that this is common knowledge? Secondly, 'far worse than what/whom?' The statement needs to be *precise* and therefore should be qualified by: 'far worse in comparison to the Australian average'. Thirdly, the student should have been *specific*: how high are the mortality (death) and morbidity (illness) rates, and what are they? Unlike everyday speech, tertiary essays are expected to be accurate, precise and specific in their content and argument.

Handy hint: use your thesaurus

The English language has a variety of words which mean similar things. Use your thesaurus to ensure you use the right word. When you find that you are over-using the same word, or would like to find a better word than the one you have come up with, look in the index of your thesaurus. Find the word you already have and the thesaurus will indicate which section to turn to. You will then find a list of options. For example, the thesaurus lists the following variations of the word *division*: separation, part, class, discord, distribution, disunity, disengagement, detachment, divorce, segregation, dislocation, split, break, section, segment, fraction, fragment . . .

Use your thesaurus!

Avoid slang, overstatements and emotive expression

Slang, overstatements and emotive expression can lead to bias and lack of clarity in your essays. All three are common in speech, but should be avoided in academic writing. Do not use slang ('rad', 'narly', 'cool') as these expressions are often culture and age specific and may create misunderstanding. For example, in the 1970s the word 'cool' did not have the slang meaning it does today (where now it is used to refer to something which is fashionable or acceptable, often used in place of the slang 'OK'), in fact, 'cool' and 'hot' can mean the same thing! Words such as 'good', 'bad', 'great', 'silly' are imprecise and emotive and should be avoided, along with the statements listed below:

'His argument is stupid'
'It was great'
'It was an awful finding'
'The paper is fabulous'
'It is a dramatic piece of evidence'

Avoid euphemisms and tautologies

Euphemisms are mild and vague phrases substituted for direct words. Euphemisms were put to great effect in the Gulf War where terms such as 'friendly fire' were used to mean 'killing your own soldiers by mistake'! Euphemisms dilute meaning and should be avoided. For example, instead of 'senior citizens', use 'the old' or 'elderly'; instead of 'passed away', use 'died'.

Tautology means repeating something that you have already said in the same sentence. Sports commentators are famous for using them! Tautologies are common in everyday speech, so watch out for them creeping into your writing, such as:

'a *decisive* decision'
'the bag was *completely* empty'
'to *revert* back'
'the *three* triplets'
'*each* and every one'
'*more* easy'

Avoid point form

Academic writing involves structured sentences and paragraphs. Unless otherwise stated, do not use point form in your essays. Point form is fine for taking notes, but part of your essay mark is based on your writing ability, that is, your ability to put your thoughts into sentences and paragraphs with the proper logical links.

9

Write it right: handling the nitty-gritty

This chapter shows you how to use abbreviations, apostrophes, tables, diagrams and appendices. These are the nitty-gritty aspects of writing, but nonetheless are important in the overall scheme of essay writing.

The nitty-gritty represents those minor aspects of writing that can often cause uncertainty, confusion and the loss of marks. It is not always possible for you to remember how to use abbreviations or tables. You may simply forget just how you are meant to use apostrophes in certain situations. This chapter should be used as a reference, to remove the cobwebs that tend to form in your mind about these aspects of writing. Whilst the nitty-gritty is a minor part of the essay writing process, it is also an area in which many easy marks can be lost.

CAREFUL USE OF ABBREVIATIONS

Abbreviations as shortened forms of words are fine for notes and drafts, but in the formal essay use the full word.

Handling the nitty-gritty.

Substitute the following words as alternatives to the abbreviations:

e.g.   for example/an example/examples include/such as
i.e.   that is/in other words
etc.   avoid its use.
       Etc. means 'and so on', which is unnecessary.

Abbreviations as acronyms

You cannot assume that everyone knows the meanings of abbreviations such as RSI, ACTU or OECD. The standard practice for such abbreviations is to write them out in full the first time you use them in your essay and give the abbreviation in brackets afterwards. From then on you can use the abbreviated form. Note that you no longer have to place full stops after each capital letter. For example:

> The Australian Council of Trade Unions (ACTU) argues that negotiations should take place. It is ACTU policy that . . .

AVOID PERSONAL EXPRESSIONS

Although it is acceptable to write from the first person point of view ('I will argue', 'In my essay I will cover'), do not use personal expressions as sentence openers, such as 'I feel', 'In my opinion', 'I believe', 'I think'. Expressions such as 'I believe' state the obvious (obviously you believe it because you are the one writing it!).

HOW TO USE APOSTROPHES

Apostrophes are used to do two things: to abbreviate missing letters and to show possession.

1. Apostrophes as abbreviations

Look at the following examples of apostrophes used as abbreviations:

> *We have arrived* can be abbreviated to *We've arrived*
> *I cannot* can be abbreviated to *I can't*
> *I will do it* can be abbreviated to *I'll do it*
> *I am here* can be abbreviated to *I'm here*

The most common mistake in using an apostrophe is in using its or it's. *It's* is short for it is. *Its* indicates the possessive.

Example:

It's better to always write it is, if you are confused about which one to use.
The dog lost *its* bone. Here *its* is used to show that the bone belongs to the dog.

---

2. Apostrophes to show possession

Students often get confused about where to put an apostrophe to show possession: should it go before or after the 's'?

For example:

> If there is one girl, *The girl's book*. The apostrophe
> shows possession—the book belongs to the girl.
> If there is more than one girl: *The girls' book*. The
> book belongs to the girls.
> If there are many books, this does not affect the use
> of the apostrophe: *The girls' books*.

Possible confusion occurs when a word, usually a name,
ends in an 's'. For example *Parsons'* theory is the theory
formulated by Parsons. In effect, what you are implying here
is *Parsons's* but adding the 's' is seen as unnecessary.

Other problems occur when people confuse plurals
with apostrophes. For example *It is the families problem*
should be *It is the family's problem*.

COMMON SPELLING MISTAKES

You will lose marks for spelling and typing mistakes. You
are expected to proofread your work and correct any
mistakes before handing your essay in. Have a dictionary
and thesaurus handy when you write your final draft. Some
words are easy to misspell, so be careful to check any
words you are unsure of. See Chapter 12 for more
information on editing your work, especially the problems
involved in using computer spellcheckers.

**Example: Some common spelling mistakes which are
easy to miss**

Incorrect	*Correct*
Relevent	Relevant
Independance	Independence
Seperate	Separate
Developement	Development

The 'i' before 'e' rule

People still get this one muddled, often because they forget the 'except after c' part so that words such as 'belief', and 'relief' lead to 'recieve' instead of 'receive'. Everybody knows this rule, but when we type or write, it often comes out wrong anyway. So always check that you've followed the rule which has been drummed into us since childhood!

The affect/effect conundrum

The difference between 'affect' (verb) and 'effect' (noun) can be subtle and confusing. If in doubt refer to your dictionary or thesaurus. The best way to understand the difference between the two words is to remember: *affect* is a verb (a doing word) and *effect* is a noun (a naming word). For example:

> affect (verb): 'The drug *affects* me' (causes a change in something)
> effect (noun): 'The drug *effects* are serious' (names what the drug does)

The which/who distinction

Only use 'who' to refer to people. Use 'that' to refer to inanimate objects such as corporations. For example:

> 'People *who* believe in . . . '
> 'Corporations *which* damage the environment . . . '

To practice or practise?

These two words are often mixed up: For example:

> practise (verb): 'The tennis players *practise* all day.'
> practice (noun): 'The law *practice* catered for all types of cases.'

AVOIDING SEXIST LANGUAGE

There are many sexist words in the English language, with expression biased toward the masculine. Be aware when you refer to both genders not to leave the other half of the population out by referring only to 'him', 'he', 'men', 'man' or 'mankind'. Do not refer to the gender of a person if it is not relevant. You can easily substitute him/her, s/he or simply write about humanity, people or individuals when you are describing both genders. The 'Handy hint' box below provides some alternatives to sexist words and expressions.

Handy hint: examples of non-sexist writing

Instead of using:	*Try:*
man/mankind	humankind, human beings, people, men and women
man in the street	the typical/average person
manmade	synthetic, artificial
chairman	chair, chairperson, head, coordinator
housewife	homemaker, houseperson, consumer
girls/ladies	women
salesman	sales representative, sales person
businessman	business executive/manager
fireman/policeman	fire fighter/police officer
cleaning lady	cleaner
actress	actor
the female doctor	the doctor

AVOIDING RACIST LANGUAGE

Note that there are no such words as 'ethnics' or an 'ethnic'. Instead use 'people of NESB' (Non-English Speaking Background), or refer specifically to the actual ethnic group if it is necessary.

To refer to the Australian indigenous population, use *Aborigine (singular noun)*, *Aborigines (plural noun)*, *Aboriginal (adjective)*. Note the use of the capital 'A' for Aborigine, as in capital 'I' for Italian. By using the lower case, such as aborigine, you are referring to the original inhabitants of *any* country. The capital 'A' identifies a specific group of people, Australian Aborigines.

CAPITALS, EMPHASIS AND ITALICS

Capitals should be used for the first letter of names of organisations, institutions and legislation. For example:
- Department of Foreign Affairs
- House of Representatives
- Act of Federal Parliament
- the Federal Government.

Note the use of the capital 'G' for government when referring to a specific entity.

When you refer to a title of a book, article or act of parliament, you need to emphasise the words. In hand-written work this can be done by underlining the titles. If you are using a typewriter or a computer, use italics to show emphasis instead. Underlining or italics should be used for:
- titles of books, journals and newspapers
- government reports
- foreign words and phrases.

Note that parliamentary acts and bills are written and emphasised in the following manner: *Telecommunication Act 1988*, *Defence Amendment Bill*, or they are underlined.

NUMBERS, DATES AND PERCENTAGES

If a number is two digits or more (10, 100) use the actual numerical form. For one digit numbers write the word for the number (five, seven). Always write the words per cent (note they are two words). The only exception to the above is that you must *write* in letters any number when it begins or ends a sentence. Dates and times should be written in the following way:

10.30 a.m.
June 25, or 25 June 1990
1990s.

Example: how to write numbers and dates

There have been many terrorist attacks on civilians in the 1990s. Twenty-five [always use a hyphen] people were killed in an explosion recently in Mexico. The death toll was 10 per cent of the people injured in the explosion. Of the survivors, five were injured seriously, with each spending an average of 20 days in hospital. The bomb exploded on July 3 at 11.30 a.m.

TABLES, FIGURES AND DIAGRAMS

Sometimes tables, diagrams and graphs are necessary to explain or enhance complex ideas or information. Specific disciplines will have their own requirements, but generally graphs, diagrams and tables should be placed in an appendix at the end of your essay. Make sure to provide each item with a heading and a reference. Including a visual representation of information should always be considered as an addition to the written part of your essay, not as a replacement for writing about the information contained in the graph, diagram or table.

How to reference

This chapter will show you the how and why of referencing. It provides examples of four different referencing systems: Harvard, American Psychological Association, footnotes and Vancouver. It shows you how to reference direct quotes, what to do when one author quotes another, and how to acknowledge books without authors and edited books, along with doing bibliographies and reference lists.

At first, referencing can seem the most confusing aspect of essay writing. However, it is simply a technique that shows the reader where you got the information you used in your essay.

REASONS FOR REFERENCING

The reasons for referencing remain the same no matter which discipline you study or method of referencing you use. In this chapter you will be introduced to four different systems of referencing. Due to tradition or professional rivalry, different disciplines use different methods. To avoid confusion, pick the referencing system preferred by the discipline for which you are writing the essay and stick to it throughout. If you are doing subjects in various disciplines, always check which referencing system you should use. Each discipline you study should provide you with specific information about how you should reference, but this chapter will address the basics.

You reference:

- for honesty and to guard against plagiarism (to ac-knowledge where you got your information)
- to give your essay credibility (to prove the source of information)
- to allow people to follow up on your sources.

Reference direct quotes and summarised information. You still have to provide a reference for information you have gathered in your own words, including:

- statistics
- research findings
- the ideas, concepts and theories of other authors.

A reference in every paragraph?

Since you must acknowledge where you get your information from, this may well mean that virtually every paragraph in your essay will have a reference in it. It is meant to. In Chapter 4 we saw that academic essays are meant to critically analyse the material on a certain topic which involves the use of referenced supporting evidence. Your marks come from your ability to find, organise and explain the relevant information. However, you will lose 'easy' marks if you fail to show the source of the information.

Warning: the dangers of plagiarism

Plagiarism is considered theft of another author's work (ideas, theories, research findings). Plagiarism occurs when another author's words and ideas are used in an essay, but are not acknowledged with an appropriate reference. Inaccurate referencing and inaccurate bibliographies will result in reduced marks. A total lack of referencing or evidence of intention not to acknowledge or to falsely acknowledge sources (plagiarism) may result in a fail. Plagiarism occurs when:

1. There is a total lack of referencing.
2. Phrases and/or sentences are used word for word without quotation marks or a reference to the author.
3. There is evidence of a deliberate intention to deceive by inventing references, or paraphrasing information from a text that is not in the bibliography or reference list.
4. Ideas and information are paraphrased (put in a student's own words), but are not referenced.
5. Part or all of the work of other students is copied.

Plagiarism is a serious offence and can lead to your expulsion from tertiary study. It can be viewed as an attempt to pass subjects fraudulently. It is up to you to ensure that your sources of information are correctly referenced. Consult your lecturer or tutor if you have any doubts as to the correct technique.

Facts which can't be checked: radio and TV

Unless it is particularly important to your essay, avoid referencing radio and television programs. Tapes of programs are not easily accessible and therefore neither is any information obtained from them for the marker to check your understanding. Additionally, there are many errors and opinions expressed as facts in the media, so avoid relying on the media as a source of information.

THE BIBLIOGRAPHY OR REFERENCE LIST

At the end of your essay you must include a list of all the sources of information you referenced in your essay. This list is called either a *reference list* or a *bibliography* (the terminology varies depending on the discipline). Aside from the Vancouver referencing system most referencing systems have a bibliography/reference list organised in alphabetical order by the surname of the first author of a book or article.

Facts which can't be checked.

It is here that you provide the full details of the books and journal articles used. In general, the list should only include the books and articles that were actually referenced in the essay. Do not include any other material that was not referenced just to make your list of references look better, unless you are specifically requested to do so.

THE HARVARD AND APA REFERENCING SYSTEMS

The most common referencing system is the Harvard or American Psychological Association (APA) system where the reference appears in the text of the essay: (Author, year: page). The Harvard and APA systems are very similar since they both reference information by providing the surname of the author, the year and page numbers in the text of your essay. All the bibliographical information (title, edition, publisher, place) appears in a list of references at the end of your essay. The major difference between the

Harvard and APA systems is in the way references are written in the reference list. This is best shown by example in the section below on bibliographies and reference lists.

Harvard and APA also differ slightly in how a reference is written in the text of your essay. Compare the following:

Harvard style: (Apple, 1995:15)
APA style: (Apple, 1995, p.15)

A sample paragraph is produced (opposite) in the Harvard style.

Handy hint: choose your style

Sometimes particular disciplines or departments require you to use a specific style when referencing, such as the APA style. However, usually your lecturers are not so fussy as to take marks off for using a comma instead of a colon. The rule of thumb to follow is to choose the style that you prefer. As long as you consistently use the same style throughout your essays, you should not encounter any problems.

Harvard and APA reference list differences

As mentioned earlier, the main differences between the two styles of referencing is the way in which the sources are recorded in the bibliography or reference list.

Example: Harvard reference list

Apple, A.N. (1995) *Sociology Today*, St Leonards: Allen & Unwin.
Apple, A.N. (1993) 'Culture and change', *Social Theory*, Vol. 5, No. 2, 1–10.
Orang, O. (1990) *History Tomorrow*, St Leonards: Allen & Unwin.

Harvard example

'Men and women are victims of their anatomy' (Apple, 1995:15). The process by which individuals learn a culture involves learning social rules and expectations of behaviour that can be divided into two stages: primary and secondary socialisation. Primary socialisation represents the influences in early childhood from the family. Secondary socialisation reflects factors external to the family, such as friends, school and the media (Apple, 1995:5–7). The information in the previous sentences is paraphrased from pages 5 to 7 from a book by Apple written in 1995. Socialisation plays an important part in adulthood through the relearning of values and norms of behaviour (resocialisation) (Orang, 1990:200). Apple (1995) is critical of Orang's conceptualisation of resocialisation, particularly in the case of immigrants entering Australia and having to be resocialised into a new culture. Apple argues that such a view is ahistorical and apolitical because it ignores government policies of assimilation and discrimination against immigrants as coercive forms of 'resocialisation' (Apple, 1990:31). Whilst Orang (1990) provides a useful description of resocialisation, his use of examples such as women re-entering the workforce after completing family 'duties' is rightly criticised by Apple as ignoring the patriarchal nature of society (Apple, 1990).

The information in the previous sentences is paraphrased from pages 5 to 7 from a book by Apple written in 1995.

Note the full stop is after the bracket.

The APA system uses full stops after the titles of books and articles, does not use quotation marks for chapter or article titles, and writes the volume number differently to the Harvard system (note there is no issue number included for APA).

Example: APA reference list

Apple, A.N. (1995) *Sociology Today*. St Leonards: Allen & Unwin.

Apple, A.N. (1993) Culture and change. *Social Theory*, 5, 1–10.

Orang, O. (1990) *History Tomorrow*. St Leonards: Allen & Unwin.

HOW TO REFERENCE IN THE HARVARD/APA STYLE

Go through the examples provided below and note some of the variations which you can use. There are two ways to write a Harvard/APA style of reference. One method is to cite the author as a part of the actual sentence (with only the year and page numbers in brackets); the other is to include the author, date and page all in brackets. Most writers use both and alternate between the two methods for variety. Both methods are acceptable and your choice of which one to use will depend on the structure of the sentence.

When there is one author

When you are referencing only one author, you can do so in a number of ways.

Apple (1995:56) states that . . .

Here the author's name is part of the sentence. The reference shows that the information came from page 56 in a book by Apple, written in 1995. Note that there is always a space between the author and the bracket.

Bryson argues that . . . (1992:10–16).

When the author's name is part of the sentence you can also place the reference at the end of the sentence. This case shows the material was written in 1992, with the information gathered from pages 10 through to 16.

It can be argued that . . . (Bryson 1992:10–16).

When the author's name is not part of the sentence, place the full reference at the end of the sentence, all in brackets, with the full stop after the bracket.

Connell (1988: 5–10, 15–20) maintains . . . .

Here the reference shows that the information has come from disconnected pages.

When there are two authors

The same method of referencing is followed when there are two authors.

Russell and Schofield (1986:6) suggest . . .

When there are two authors, cite them like this; there is no need to include initials.

There is evidence to suggest . . . (Russell and Schofield 1986:6).

As with single authors, place a bracketed reference at the end of the sentence when the author names are not part of the sentence.

Citing multiple authors

Sometimes you may summarise the findings or views of a number of different works. When this is the case, you can include all the different authors in the one reference in the following way:

A number of authors have found . . . (Bryson, 1992; Connell, 1988; Legge and Westbrook, 1994).

Note that a semi-colon separates the different authors.

When there are three or more authors

You can use the abbreviation *et al.* (note the lower case, full stop and italics) when there are three or more authors. Whenever you use a foreign word, even an abbreviation, you need to highlight it by either using italics or underlining it.

> *Peterson* et al. *(1992:101) claim that . . .*

The Latin abbreviation, *et al.* (*et alii*), means 'and others'. The *et al.* is placed after the name of the first author. The names of the other authors can be found in the reference list at the end of your essay.

> *Studies suggest . . . (Peterson* et al. *1992:101).*

Again, when the authors are not mentioned in the sentence, then the reference can come at the end.

How to reference two or more sources by the same author

Sometimes you will use a number of sources from the same author, or there will be two sources written by different people with the same surname. If you have books or articles written in the same year by either the same person or authors with the same surname, you can distinguish between the two by placing a lower case letter, starting with 'a', after the year of publication.

> *Apple (1988a:56) states . . .*
> *Apple (1988b:23) argues . . .*

In your reference list, you will also need to provide the other bibliographical information on titles, publisher and place of publication, but remember to include the letters next to the dates so that readers can work out which reference is which.

How to reference government reports and books without authors

Some sources of information such as government reports, books published by the Australian Bureau of Statistics or the World Bank have no identifiable author. The rule to follow in these cases is to reference whoever produced the report or book. Look on the inside cover of the publication, find which organisation is responsible and reference it (for an example see below). In some cases the identity of the organisation may not be clear; therefore, all you can use is the actual title of the source and the year it was published. Remember, referencing should enable other people to find the source you used, so provide them with enough information to do this. For example, if you used a government report which had no author, but was published by the Department of Industrial Relations, you would reference it in the following way:

In your essay:
(Department of Industrial Relations, 1994).

Reference list:
Department of Industrial Relations (1994) *Best Practice: Achieving Success*, Canberra:AGPS.

When there is no obvious author

In the above example, if the report had no identifiable source, it could be written as follows:

——(1994) *Best Practice: Achieving Success*, Canberra: AGPS.

All books, reports and articles without authors should be grouped together either at the start or end of your bibliography or reference list.

How to reference newspapers

For newspapers, state the paper's name (in italics or underlined) and the date: (*The Australian*, 1 April 1996). If the article in the newspaper has an author, then use the name of the author instead of the name of the paper, for example: (Knewitt, 1995). You do not need to include page numbers when you reference newspaper articles.

In the reference list, newspaper articles should be referenced as in the example below:

> Knewitt, I. (1995) 'Higher education stress', *The Sydney Morning Herald*, 1 April.

HOW TO COMPILE A BIBLIOGRAPHY OR REFERENCE LIST

At the end of your essay you must include a list of all the sources of information you referenced in your essay. The list of books at the end of the essay is either called a *Reference list* or a *Bibliography* (the terminology varies depending on the discipline). Aside from the Vancouver referencing system (described below), most referencing systems have a bibliography or reference list organised in alphabetical order by surname of the first author of a book or article. It is here that you provide the full details of the books and journal articles used. In general, the list should only include the books and articles that were actually referenced in the essay. Do not include any other material that was not referenced, just to make your list of references look better, unless you are specifically requested to do so. Your reference list should use the following format.

Example: How to write a Harvard reference list

Bestbet, M.Y. (1996) 'How to bribe lecturers', *The Journal of Getting Away With Murder*, Vol. 6, No. 2, 191–212.

For journal articles: author's surname, date, title of article (in single quotation marks, journal title (italics or underlined), volume number, issue number, first and last page numbers of the article.

Wish, I. (1995) *How to Get Great Marks Without Really Trying*, Second edition, Sydney: Allens.

For books: author's surname, date, book title (in italics or underlined), the edition (if other than first edition, see 'Handy hint' box below), place of publication, publisher.

Youlater, C. (1995) 'Vampires: a textual analysis', B. Cause (ed.) *Vampires: Postmodermist and Marxist Critiques*, Melbourne: Winkwink.

For chapters from edited books: author's surname, date, chapter title in single quotation marks, names of editors (initials first), eds. (abbreviation for editors), book title in italics, place of publication and publisher.

Handy hint: editions, impressions and reprints

If there is more than one edition of a book, always include the edition number in your reference list. There is no need to record that a book is a first edition. Different editions of a book mean that some of the content and layout has changed (page numbers and content in one edition may no longer correspond with an earlier edition). Therefore, it is important to record the edition of the book you used in your reference list or bibliography. *Note that impressions and reprints are not new editions* (they signify the reprinting of a book if the previous print run has sold out) and there is no need to note them in the bibliography/reference list.

THE FOOTNOTE METHOD

Footnotes are a different way of referencing your information. Footnoting means inserting a number at the end of a sentence for each reference. You then provide the corresponding bibliographic information in the form of a note at the foot of the page or at the end of the essay (endnotes) before the reference list. Either way, you mark the numbers consecutively in the order in which the references appear in the essay (for example, from 1 to 30), never repeating a number.

The first reference to a book or article in a footnote must provide the same full bibliographic details as you would provide in a bibliography or reference list. After that, if you reference the same book or article, you can use Latin abbreviations such as those below:

- *ibid.* (short for *ibidem*, meaning 'in the same place')
- *op. cit.* (short for *opere citato*, meaning 'in the work cited').
- short title.

See the example below on how to footnote, especially using Latin abbreviations. The abbreviation *ibid.* is used to refer to the same book or article as the one noted in the reference immediately before it. The abbreviation *op. cit.* is used to reference the same book or article that has already been referenced in full in the essay, but does not directly follow from the one above. Always remember to include the name of the author along with the *op. cit.* to avoid any confusion. Note that when you use either abbreviation you should use the lower case, include the full stops and either underline or italicise the Latin words.

When there is more than one book or article by the same author, the short title abbreviation is used. The short title abbreviation (footnote 7 in the example below) can also be used as a simple alternative to the Latin abbreviations.

Footnote example

'*Men and women are victims of their anatomy*'.[1] *The process by which individuals learn a culture involves learning social rules and expectations of behaviour that can be divided into two stages: primary and secondary socialisation. Primary socialisation represents the influences in early childhood from the family. Secondary socialisation reflects factors external to the family, such as friends, school and the media.*[2] *Socialisation plays an important part in adulthood through the relearning of values and norms of behaviour (resocialisation).*[3] *Apple is critical of Orang's conceptualisation of resocialisation, particularly in the case of immigrants entering Australia and having to be resocialised into a new culture.*[4] *Apple argues that such a view is ahistorical and apolitical because it ignores government policies of assimilation and discrimination against immigrants as coercive forms of 'resocialisation'.*[5] *Whilst Orang provides a useful description of resocialisation, his use of examples such as women re-entering the workforce after completing family 'duties' is rightly criticised by Apple as ignoring the patriarchal nature of society.*[6,7]

---

1. Apple, A.N. (1995) *Sociology Today*, Sydney, Allen & Unwin, p. 15
2. *ibid.*, pp. 5–7
3. Orang, O. (1990) *History Tomorrow*, Sydney, Allen & Unwin, p. 200
4. Apple, A.N. (1993) 'Culture and change', *Social Theory*, Vol. 5, No. 2, 1–10.
5. *ibid.*
6. Orang, *op. cit.*, p. 201
7. Apple, *Social Theory*, p. 31 (the short title alternative to using *ibid.* and *op. cit.*)

THE VANCOUVER SYSTEM

The Vancouver referencing system is common amongst the health sciences. It involves the use of endnotes, but differs greatly from the footnoting system. It is the simplest but least detailed of the four systems of referencing discussed in this book. In the Vancouver system, the endnotes and reference list are one and the same. In essence, you construct a list of references or bibliography of all the books and articles used in the essay, and number them in the order in which they appear. Therefore, the number of each reference in the text refers to the reference at the end of the essay. Note that article titles are often abbreviated using a form published in the catalogue *Index Medicus* (available in your library). In the example below, the reference list is numbered and corresponds to the numbers in the text of your essay.

The Vancouver system is less page specific that the Harvard, APA or footnote methods. It also involves a different method of writing the references in the reference list. Books and journal articles are not italicised or highlighted in any way, nor are any Latin abbreviations used. There are no quotation marks used for article or chapter titles.

Vancouver example

'Men and women are victims of their anatomy'.[1] The process by which individuals learn a culture involves learning social rules and expectations of behaviour that can be divided into two stages: primary and secondary socialisation. Primary socialisation represents the influences in early childhood from the family. Secondary socialisation reflects factors external to the family, such as friends, school and the media.[1] Socialisation plays an important part in adulthood through the relearning of

values and norms of behaviour (resocialisation).² Apple is critical of Orang's conceptualisation of resocialisation, particularly in the case of immigrants entering Australia and having to be resocialised into a new culture.³ Apple argues that such a view is ahistorical and apolitical because it ignores government policies of assimilation and discrimination against immigrants as coercive forms of 'resocialisation'.³ Whilst Orang provides a useful description of resocialisation, his use of examples such as women re-entering the workforce after completing family 'duties' is rightly criticised by Apple as ignoring the patriarchal nature of society.²,³

References

1. Apple A.N. Sociology Today. Sydney, Allen & Unwin, 15–32, 1995.
2. Orang O. History Tomorrow. Sydney, Allen & Unwin, 1990.
3. Apple, A.N. Culture and change. Social Theory 1993; 5(2): 1–10.

Handy hint: do not mix your referencing systems

Do not confuse the four systems of referencing. For example, do not mix footnotes with Harvard-style citations or Vancouver-style numbering. The footnoting method does not require dates next to the names of authors when mentioned in the text of an essay.

USING DIRECT QUOTES

Direct quotes (word for word) from authors should be kept to a minimum (no more than 10 per cent of the essay). Do not make your essay into a chain of quotes. It

Don't mix your referencing systems.

is impossible to assess whether you have understood what you have read if you do not use your own words. Re-phrase your material in your own words and provide references. With direct quotes that are shorter than 30 words:

- use quotation marks
- always give page number(s).

If a direct quote is longer than 30 words, indent the quote from each margin and use single spacing if typed. There is no need to use quotation marks when indenting. The example below shows a long direct quote that has been indented:

Russell and Schofield (1986:16) state:

the fact remains that the most significant improvements in mortality occurred *independently* of medical therapies, and death rates have remained substantially unchanged since the 1930s. Yet we have been spending more and more or health *services* during the past 50 yers [sic].

The use of 'sic' and added information in direct quotes

Sometimes the direct quotes you use will have mistakes in them (as the one above). You still have to reproduce the direct quote with the mistake, but you identify the mistake as belonging to the original source by using the abbreviation [sic]. Note that sic is surrounded by *square* brackets. To make a direct quote make sense in your paragraph, you may need to add a few words to make the quote fit the tense of your sentence or to define a word for clarification. In both cases, this is done with the use of square brackets, which denote you have added something to the original direct quote. Whilst it is acceptable for you to do this, you must be careful to ensure you do not alter the meaning of the original direct quote in the process (see the example below).

The three dots (ellipsis)

In a direct quote, you may wish to shorten the original version by cutting some words from it, to save space or eject irrelevant information. You can do this using ellipsis. Taking the same direct quote as above, you could shorten it in the following way:

Russell and Schofield (1986:16) state:

the fact remains that the most significant improvements in mortality occurred *independently* of medical therapies, and death rates have remained substantially unchanged . . . [but we are] spending more and more on health *services* . . .

Note that there is no need for an extra full stop after the three dots.

Remember, always use the exact wording and grammar, even *italics*, when directly quoting. Be careful not to change the meaning of the quote by using it out of context.

The quote within a quote: when one author quotes another

When one author quotes another and you want to use the same direct quote, there is a simple rule to follow. For example, Willis is the author of the book you are using and he has used a direct quote from Smith, which you also want to use. The rule to follow is always reference where *you* got the information, that is, from Willis. The examples below show you two ways to reference when one author quotes another:

> Smith (quoted in Willis, 1993:12) states: 'social problems cannot be blamed on individuals alone'.

> It is argued that: 'social problems cannot be blamed on individuals alone' (Smith cited in Willis, 1993:12).

Choose either 'quoted in' or 'cited in' and be consistent with its use. *Warning*: use this method only with a direct quote. If Willis only summarised the work of Smith in his own words you do not mention Smith at all; instead reference Willis.

Handy hint: referencing checklist

- are your references in alphabetical order? (Applies to Harvard, APA and footnote systems)
- are all the authors in the text of your essay listed in your reference list/bibliography?
- are all the bibliographic details provided: authors, dates, titles, publishers, places?
- do you have the journal volume, number and page details?

Common reasons for losing marks over poor referencing:

- a direct quotation without quotation marks and/or a page reference
- omission of necessary references. As a general rule each paragraph in a first year essay should have at least one reference (except the introduction and the conclusion)
- inaccurate referencing, such as wrong year, wrong page number, wrong text
- sloppy technique, such as omitting the date or page numbers
- sloppy bibliography/reference list, such as date in the wrong place, titles not underlined or italicised, omission of vital bibliographic information or inconsistency of technique used.
- made up references. Never falsify a reference by thinking of a fake author and source. If it is discovered by a marker, it is grounds for automatic failure.

11

Other types of writing

This chapter shows you how to write book and article reviews, abstracts, summaries, reports and exam essays.

Other types of writing.

BOOK AND ARTICLE REVIEWS

A common piece of written assessment is the book or article review. This involves you reading, summarising and analysing a particular book or article within a set word limit. You should treat a review like an essay. It should have an introduction, use supporting evidence, have a conclusion and be referenced.

There are two parts to a review: the descriptive summary and the analysis of the material you are reviewing. You gain marks by showing that you understand what the book or article is about, and that you have been able to link it into wider debates in the existing literature. The important point to remember is that you are explaining what the author is saying, rather than merely describing and repeating the words of the author. The key aspect of a review is the evaluation of the strengths and weaknesses of the particular work. Much of your analysis will be derived from other sources of information and you are therefore often expected to do wider reading on the topic.

After your introduction, you should describe the main points of the work in terms of its content and its argument. The descriptive part of the review should not take up more than 50 per cent of the overall word limit. The remainder of the review should be set aside for analysis: this is where you evaluate what the author argues, indicating strengths and weaknesses such as the quality of the supporting evidence for arguments and the importance of the issues raised.

In reviews, the following format can be used as a general guide:

1. Title page, with full details of the name of author(s), date, title, place and publisher of the work to be reviewed.

2. An introductory paragraph which includes the full name of the author and the title of the book or article.

3. In the introduction, briefly describe what the work is about, the author's central argument or theoretical perspective.
4. Then proceed to describe and critically analyse the article.
5. In one paragraph, write a conclusion which sums up the material and provides an overall evaluation of the article in terms of its central argument and its relevance to the field of study.
6. You are required to reference the article you are reviewing as you would in an essay, and it therefore appears in your reference list at the end of your assignment.

ABSTRACTS AND SUMMARIES

An abstract is a brief overview of an essay, article or piece of research in usually no more than 200 words. It is useful to think of the abstract as an essay in one paragraph. Abstracts are meant to:

- introduce the reader to the topic
- briefly note the literature, theories and methods consulted (where relevant)
- state the findings, argument and/or conclusions
- be no longer than 200 words (unless otherwise specified).

A good way to write an abstract of an article is to sum up each paragraph in a sentence. You then have to make sense of the sentences and link them together. In many cases, one sentence per paragraph will give you too much information for an abstract. You will then need to cut out what is unnecessary by determining what the key theme or argument of the article is and only including the sentences that are relevant.

A summary serves the same purpose as an abstract, but is often considerably greater in length. You will normally be asked to write summaries of articles or chapters. A summary is a descriptive piece of writing which should cover the main content, argument and theoretical perspective (if applicable) of the work being summarised. Summaries are often used as minor assessment tasks to enforce course reading requirements and to give evidence that you understand the reading and can determine and summarise the important points. When writing a summary, summarise the information in your own words and avoid using direct quotes.

REPORTS

Each discipline or subject sets specific report formats for you to follow. Always follow these formats exactly because often a certain percentage of the marks for a report is awarded for presentation and using the correct format. Reports are usually written for research or lab-based assignments. Whilst report writing is different from essay writing, the techniques described earlier for planning, researching and organising your material still apply. Report formats use subheadings to divide the text and make more use of tabulated and diagrammatic presentation of information. The nature of report formats varies depending on the discipline and the assignment. Use the following guidelines as a checklist:

Report title: provides a good description of what the report is about.

Abstract: separated from the rest of the text on a separate page (see section above).

Introduction: provides a brief discussion of the problem or topic being dealt with.

Literature review: a brief review of the literature (described and analysed).

Research question: a clear statement of the research question or problem. Sometimes this is included in the introduction to the report.

Methodology: provide a description of the when, where and how of the study. Include information on the sample (number of subjects, where they were recruited and how they were selected); the data collection techniques used (interviews, surveys, observation, experiments); and how the data was processed, presented and analysed.

Results (and discussion): the data is presented in the results section which describes the findings. Some report formats allow you to combine the results and the discussion, whilst others prefer the two sections to be dealt with separately.

Discussion and conclusions: analyse the results by linking them to the existing empirical and theoretical literature that you summarised in the literature review. Keep the research question in mind and make some conclusions based on the data. Also note any problems encountered and possibilities for improvement of the study or areas for future research.

Provide a **list of references**.

EXAM ESSAYS

The key to exam essays is preparation, both before and during the actual exam. Exam essays are meant to follow the same conventions as normal student essays. They should have an introduction, a body and a conclusion. Exam essays must attempt to answer the essay question by showing your knowledge of the subject matter and your ability to analyse the topic by explaining various issues or applying relevant theories. Be as detailed as your memory allows, but there is no need to reference your material.

Success in exam essays is based on your preparation. Prior to the exam, prepare your lecture and reading notes by summarising them under key headings. A good way to prepare before an exam essay is to *practise with sample questions or past exam papers* which lecturers may make available. If there is no access to sample questions, think of some yourself and test yourself by attempting a question in the same time frame as you are given in the exam.

Exam essays are meant to be written with full sentences and proper use of grammar. Only if you run out of time in an exam should you list what you were going to say in point form. If you have messy writing, use print rather than a cursive style. There are many books on the market to help you with exam study and technique, so seek out these books if you need further help.

Memory joggers

During an exam, preparation is vital. Before you begin to write, use all the essay planning strategies discussed earlier in this book. Make a plan of your exam essay. Look for command and key words in the question and make sure you address them in the essay. Do some mindmapping and even mindclearing if needed.

A good way to brainstorm an exam essay is to use certain words as 'memory joggers'. When you study for the exam, summarise the main theories and facts under easily remembered words. These words can act as memory joggers in the exam. Once you think of the word, it conjures up a whole host of related material. In the exam essay planning stage, record all the relevant memory joggers you can think of that relate to the topic. Do not waste time trying to write down a whole host of detailed facts. In exams, you do not have time to write a draft, so the memory joggers save you time by allowing you to plan your essay quickly. The detailed sentences and facts will flow as you begin to write your exam essay by using the memory joggers and your mindmap as prompts for your writing.

The memory jogger.

Handy hint: exam technique

The most common reason for students doing badly in exams when they know the content is that they do not allocate time correctly. Always keep a note of the time and apportion the time required to complete your exam questions according to the marks or weighting of particular items. For example, if there are two exam essay questions, with one worth 60 per cent and the other 40 per cent of the total mark, divide the time spent on each essay in the same way. That is, 60 per cent of the exam time should be spent on the 60 per cent essay. Be disciplined with your time allocation.

12

Typing and proofreading your work

Once you have written your essay it is time to do some editing and polishing so that the final version is submitted as a truly finished product. This chapter gives you tips on how to proofread your essay.

TO TYPE OR NOT TO TYPE?

The preference of any marker is a typed essay. If you have the option of using a computer, then use it! From a marker's point of view, the typed essay is much easier to read and mark than the hieroglyphics that pass for some students' handwriting. If you cannot type or do not have access to a computer, make sure you take the time to write your essay clearly. Preferably print the essay to ensure that it is easier to read. After putting in the effort to research the essay, it would be a pity if you lost marks because it was impossible to read your 'individual' writing style.

USING COMPUTERS

Even if you do not have a personal computer, most tertiary institutions now provide access to computers for students. If you can afford it, it is worth considering investing in a computer. Not only will computer experience enhance your employment skills, it will make your life easier, especially for writing essays. Typing and rearranging notes, compiling references, cutting and pasting various sentences or paragraphs from one part of the essay to another and spellchecking are all made much easier with a computer. Once you know how to use a computer, it will save you time in your essay writing.

There are now many avenues to learn how to use computers, from hundreds of books to short courses (many run by tertiary institutions). However, if you use a computer, you should also be aware of its limitations, some of which are highlighted below.

Prepare for the crash

No matter how careful you are with your computer or how expensive the equipment, eventually all computer users will experience the dreaded crash. This is where your computer jams, your disk becomes corrupt, or your work is not saved before you exit the program. There are a multitude of possibilities that can result in your hard work being lost. The general safety rule with using computers is to treat each time you use a computer as a potential time for a crash to occur. In other words, always take precautions. If you are spending a long time on the computer, either typing or editing, re-save your document regularly (every 10 minutes). Always have two copies of your document, a 'back-up' on floppy disk and one on the hard drive. By making back-up copies you avoid losing your essay.

A computer crash is no excuse for not submitting an essay on time. The onus is on you to take the precautions.

However, this does not stop some students from using, rightly or wrongly, a whole range of excuses for not submitting an essay on time, or for not picking up mistakes. See the 'Handy hint' box for a list of updated versions of 'the dog ate it'.

Beware of the limits of spellcheckers

Typing invariably produces typing mistakes. If you rely on a computer to check your spelling for you, be aware that the computer will not find correctly spelled words used inappropriately. Sometimes such words will be the result of typing mistakes, such as typing *the* instead of *them*, so be aware that spellchecking is only a stage prior to proofreading. Spellcheckers are very useful, but they do not do all the work for you.

The limits of spellcheckers.

Handy hint: avoiding the top ten computer excuses

The computer crashed.
The disk is stuffed.
I lost the disk.
I didn't keep a disk copy.
The printer jammed.
My friend's disk gave my computer a virus.
The printer ribbon ran out.
There was a power blackout in my area.
My typing skills aren't that good.
My spellchecker didn't pick it up.

Computer excuses.

PROOFREADING: THE LAST IMPORTANT TASK

After you have finished your essay, it is common to experience feelings of satisfaction and relief. The essay is finally done and the pressure is off. Most students do not spend enough time proofreading their finished essays. Some make the mistake of relying on their spellcheckers, whilst others just don't do it at all. Some students have submitted their essay without proofreading, only to find that pages are out of order, references are incorrect, or the printer was misaligned. If you take the time to check the final version of your essay, you will usually find some mistakes which can easily be corrected and will save you marks.

The following example should sound familiar to you, and is common where students have not done their proofreading. Often when you write out the final version of your essay, you fix up some of the sentence structure and expression along the way. It is not uncommon for a word to be on the 'tip of your tongue', but it refuses to pop out, so you leave a space for the word, making a mental note to come back to it later. A variation on this theme is an essay full of correction fluid gaps. You find a mistake, or you make a mistake as you are writing and use correction fluid. Since it takes a while to dry, you continue to write (not wanting to break your creative flow), making a mental note to come back to it. In both cases, it is easy to forget these mental notes and hand in an essay with white blanks on the pages.

Proofreading is not easy, so don't think you can rush it. Mistakes are easy to miss even when you are looking for them. You are usually so familiar with the material by the time you have finished your essay that when you begin to read through it, your mind anticipates what is to come and you begin to gloss over what you are reading. The simplest way to overcome such proofreading pitfalls is to get a friend or family member to proofread your work. If you go it alone, the only way to ensure you do not miss mistakes is to read your essay line by line. Block all the lines of your essay, bar the one you are actually reading, with a ruler or piece of paper. Concentrate on each word in the line, moving to the next but keeping the others covered. Line by line is the only sure way to do it.

13

The end . . . or just the beginning

This chapter gives you an indication of how essays are assessed, makes you aware of your rights as a student and provides a final essay pre-submission checklist.

Your detective work is just about over and the verdict on your investigation will soon be delivered. It's now time to consider just what markers expect and just how your essay is likely to be assessed. As an academic detective you've learnt to look for clues, analyse various theories and support what you say with credible evidence. However, you may have got a little too close to your subject matter. The only way to ensure your judgment has stayed accurate is never to assume that everyone knows what you now know.

THE ESSAY PRE-SUBMISSION CHECKLIST

Before you hand in your essay, check for the following:
1. Unless you are specifically asked, do not place your essays in expensive folders and folios. Often all these

do is frustrate your lecturers/tutors who have to lug them around and dismantle them in order to read your essay. Save money and the environment.

2. The cover sheet to your essay should contain the essay question, your name, your tutor's name, tutorial time, subject name, course code and due date.
3. Preferably type your essay. Type or write on one side of the paper only and leave a wide margin (4 centimetres) for marker's comments.
4. Use double spacing for typed work.
5. Always include a bibliography or reference list.
6. Avoid including graphs and tables in your essay, unless you are specifically asked to do so. If you need to use them, put them in an appendix at the back of your essay (with a reference), before the bibliography or reference list.
7. Staple the pages of your essay together, avoid using pins or paper clips.
8. *Keep a copy of your essay (just in case it goes astray).* The onus is on YOU to prove you have done the work, even if the assignment is lost after it is submitted.

NEVER ASSUME: KEEP IT SIMPLE

Your essay marker knows the subject well, but it is up to you to prove that you do too. Forget for a moment that the marker knows the essay topic back to front and instead imagine you handed your essay to someone on the street for marking. Therefore, you need to define and explain all the terms, concepts and theories you use. A good test of the clarity of your writing is to let your friends or family read your essay and ask them to point out anything they do not understand. Sometimes what is in your head does not make it to paper. It is easy to become so involved in the writing process that you over-summarise your material because you assume the reader knows what you mean. Think again! The marker can only mark what is on paper.

Keep it simple.

He or she is marking *your* understanding of the issues, not what's in your head!

MARKER EXPECTATIONS: HOW YOUR WORK IS ASSESSED

It is important to have a clear idea of the expectations of your markers, particularly when it comes to assessment. Therefore, it is crucial that you follow any guidelines that are set within a subject. However, if you are unclear about what is expected of you, make some time to consult your lecturer or tutor. This book has aimed to give you a foundation for what is generally expected of a tertiary essay. Some typical comments from markers are listed in the 'Handy hint' box below. Keep them in mind and if they sound familiar, go back over the relevant parts of this book so that you can avoid such comments in the future.

Handy hint: typical critical comments from markers of essays

'Too descriptive. Explain and analyse your material.'
'Too general and vague.'
'Not enough depth or detail.'
'Wider reading was required.'
'Parts of the essay were not relevant to the question.'
'You did not answer the question.'
'Poor referencing.'
'Poor expression.'

THE MARKING SYSTEM

Most tertiary education institutions are standardising their marking systems. The standard marking system used is:

High Distinction (HD) 85% and over
Distinction (D) 75 to 84%
Credit (C) 65 to 74%
Pass (P) 50 to 64%
Fail (F) 49% and below

Where there is more than one piece of assessment, the final mark for most subjects is based on the cumulative mark or total of all the individual pieces of assessment. However, some subjects set their pass marks higher than 50 per cent, sometimes as high as 95 per cent, when there can be no room for error. This often occurs in profession based subjects, such as nursing and medicine, where competency levels must be reached (such as for drug knowledge and administration).

APPLYING FOR EXTENSIONS

If you have a legitimate problem which prevents you finishing your essay by the due date, go to your lecturer or tutor as soon as possible to request written permission for an extension. Remember, the key to a successful essay is good preparation, which means starting several weeks before it is due. Being ill the week before a due date should only delay the preparation of your final draft. Show your lecturer or tutor what you have done so far, so she or he can see that the need for your extension is not just due to bad planning. Adhere strictly to the new due date. Be aware that most lecturers and tutors have heard every excuse. There are only so many grandmothers that can possibly die (the most popular excuse) in any one semester! It is not

A final word.

uncommon for academics to ask for proof of your excuse in the form of a doctor's or counsellor's certificate. Always try to apply for an extension before the due date.

STUDENT RIGHTS

Most tertiary institutions in cooperation with student unions, are in the process of adopting and adhering to a charter of student rights. The list of rights below should be considered reasonable and basic rights concerning essays. Nonetheless, it is always best to clarify these rights with your particular lecturer/tutor, discipline or institution.

Handy hint: know your rights

- Students have a right to receive essay topics at least a month in advance of the due date.
- Students have a right to written comments along with their grade.
- Students have a right to have their essays returned within a month of submission.
- Students have a right to discuss their essays and essay plans with their tutors.
- Students have a right to a re-mark of their essay.
- Students have a right to know who marked their essay.
- Students have a right to know the 'pass' mark for the essay and the subject overall.

A FINAL WORD: GOODBYE AND GOOD LUCK!

You've made it! You now know the rules of the essay writing game. Welcome to the academic detective club; you are now a lifetime member. This book has given you the raw data on essay writing; it is now up to you to use all of the insights, hints and skills to go forth into the world of academic knowledge. Lord Bacon said that 'knowledge is power', but knowledge is useless if you can't communicate it in an understandable and convincing way. The essay is a tool for communicating your knowledge and your understanding. So as you roll the dice for the next essay game you play, remember to take your bag of detective skills with you. Enjoy the game, and good luck!

Raw data.

Further reading

There are many books available through libraries and bookshops that can help you with writing and studying. Below is a list of some of the books I find useful. Some cover similar material to this book and others include wider aspects of writing or being a student, such as how to study effectively and how to get the most out of tutorials.

——(1995) *Style Manual for Authors, Editors and Printers*, 5th edn, Canberra: AGPS.

Anderson, J. and Poole, M. (1994) *Thesis and Assignment Writing*, 2nd edn, Milton: John Wiley.

Bailey, R. F. (1984) *A Survival Kit for Writing English*, 2nd edn, Melbourne: Longman

Bate, D. and Sharpe, P. (1984) *Essay Method and English Expression*, Sydney: Harcourt Brace Jovanovich.

Burdess, N. (1991) *The Handbook of Student Skills for the Social Sciences and Humanities*, Australia: Prentice Hall.

Buzan, T. (1993) *The Mind Map Book*, London: BBC Books.

Clanchy, J. and Ballard, B. (1994) *Essay Writing for Students*, 3rd edn, Melbourne: Longman.

Fogg, C. (1994) *Mastering the Maze: How to Use Your Library to Break the Information Barrier*, Sydney: Australian Centre for Independent Journalism.

Hall, W.C. (1985) *Being a Successful Student*, Australia: Longman Cheshire.

Howe, A. (1986) *How to Study*, Great Britain: Kogan Page.

Lewins, F. (1993) *Writing a Thesis*, Canberra: Bibliotech.

Marshall, L. and Rowland, F. (1993) *A Guide to Learning Independently*, 2nd edn, Melbourne: Longman.

Murray-Smith, S. (1988) *Right Words: A Guide to English Usage in Australia*, Melbourne: Viking.

Northedge, A. (1990) *The Good Study Guide*, Milton Keynes: Open University Press.

Osland, D., Boyd, D., McKenna, W. and Salusinszky, I. (1991) *Writing in Australia*, Marrickville: Harcourt Brace Jovanovich.

Turney, C. and Teo, R. (1994) *You Can Make It: A Guide to Successful Transition to University*, St. Ives: Sydmac Academic Press.

Index